Dark
Laughter

DARK
LAUGHTER
War in Song and Popular Culture

LES CLEVELAND

PRAEGER

Westport, Connecticut
London

Library of Congress Cataloging-in-Publication Data

Cleveland, Les.
   Dark laughter : war in song and popular culture / Les Cleveland.
     p.   cm.
   Includes bibliographical references and index.
   ISBN 0–275–94764–5
   1. War songs—History and criticism. 2. Folk songs, English—
History and criticism. 3. Folk music—History and criticism.
   I. Title.
   ML3545.C54   1994
   782.42′1599—dc20   93–26432

British Library Cataloguing in Publication Data is available.

Library of Congress Catalog Card Number: 93–26432
ISBN: 0–275–94764–5

First published in 1994

Praeger Publishers, 88 Post Road West, Westport, CT 06881
An imprint of Greenwood Publishing Group, Inc.

Printed in the United States of America

The paper used in this book complies with the
Permanent Paper Standard issued by the National
Information Standards Organization (Z39.48–1984).

10 9 8 7 6 5 4 3 2

This book is dedicated to all rank-and-file infantry soldiers, especially those who fought in the Middle East and Italy in World War 2.

Contents

Preface

This book has its origins in the author's adventures as a young soldier in World War 2. For four and a half years he served in the New Zealand Army, and for much of that time as an infantryman in various formations of the Second New Zealand Expeditionary Force (2NZEF). This force was involved in operations in the Pacific, the Middle East and Italy. The components of it that campaigned in the Middle East and Italy saw the heaviest fighting and are referred to throughout this work as the N.Z. Division. With a peak strength of more than 20,000, it really amounted to a small national army with a very powerful offensive capacity since it was a self-contained force with its own transport, armor and artillery. It played a leading part in the British Eighth Army campaigns in North Africa and in the grueling struggles that accompanied the Allied advance up the Italian peninsula. Life in an infantry platoon in one of its typical battalions was uncertain and violent on account of the Division's fighting record and heavy casualty rate, but there were compensations in rough comradeship and the enjoyment of festive spells out of the line.

On these occasions there was usually a good deal of noisy tomfoolery and ribald song. In those days there were no portable tape recorders or television sets, and radio receivers were scarce and cumbersome. There were films, concert parties and instrumental groups as well as opportunities for rest and recreation at soldiers' clubs and welfare organizations behind the lines, but most of the time when they were not in combat, the troops had to amuse themselves. The platoon had a repertoire of the popular songs of the day as well as an oral culture that included material circulating through the British and Commonwealth armies, in addition to much parody and satire that originated in the N.Z. Division itself.

The present work contains selections from a World War 2 song collection made by the writer, but also includes material from World War 1 as well as from the U.S. and other sources. Access to this material was made possible through the generosity of the Smithsonian Institution. A Senior Research Fellowship with the Division of Military History at the National Museum of American History in Washington, D.C., enabled much of the research for this book to be completed.

The songs and prose narratives cited throughout this work come from a variety of sources that include a number of folksong archives in the United States. These are the Archive of Folk Culture in the American Folklife Center at the Library of Congress in Washington, D.C. (hereafter cited as LC); the Army Songs Collection in the Folklife Institute at the University of Indiana, Bloomington (cited as Indiana); the Department of Library Special Collections Folklife Archives at Western Kentucky University, Bowling Green, Kentucky (cited as Western Kentucky); the Archives of the Folklore Program at the University of California at Berkeley (cited as Berkeley); and the Vietnam Veterans Oral History and Folklore Project in the Department of Anthropology, State University College at Buffalo, New York (cited as Buffalo).

Major collections that have been consulted include the compilation of military folklore made after World War 2 by Agnes N. Underwood at Albany, New York. This work is now lodged with the Vietnam Veterans Oral History and Folklore Project at Buffalo. A descriptive account of its contents is given in Cleveland (1987). Here it is cited as the Underwood Collection. Another collection of military songs was made around 1947 by the English Department at Hamilton College in New York State and deposited in the college library. This is cited as the Hamilton Collection.

The folksong collection made by Robert W. Gordon, the first director of the Archive of Folk Culture at the Library of Congress from 1928 to 1932, has also been consulted. Gordon did extensive fieldwork, ran a column in a popular magazine called *Adventure* and acquired a great deal of information from the correspondence this generated. His collections are preserved in the present American Folklife Center at the Library of Congress. References to it in this study are cited as the Gordon Collection. Some items containing expressions thought at the time to be sensitive were filed by Gordon in a special category he called "the Inferno." References to this grouping are cited as the Gordon "Inferno."

This book also draws on songs located in the Lansdale Collection, a series of tape recordings containing songs that were sung by American personnel and others involved in the Vietnam War during the 1960s and 1970s. They were collected by General Edward G. Lansdale, who headed the Senior Liaison Office team of advisory officials in Vietnam. They have been deposited at two locations. The first is the Archive of Folk Culture in the American Folklife Center at the Library of Congress. The two tapes deposited there are cited here as Lansdale (1967) and Lansdale (1976), respectively. The second location is the Hoover Institution on War, Revolution and Peace, where duplicates of Lansdale (1967 and 1976) have been deposited along with 132 other tapes and a large collection of papers. These materials are cited as the Edward G. Lansdale Collection in the Hoover Institution Archives at Stanford.

Occasional references are made to songs, unpublished letters, diaries and other papers in the author's personal collection of materials relating to the general field of military song and popular culture. These are held at the writer's home in Wellington, New Zealand, and are cited here as the Cleveland Collection.

Numerous compilations of military songs have been published during the last seventy-five years, but most of them lack detail about sources and have little to say about the circumstances under which the songs were performed. None of them makes much attempt to discuss the social meaning of this body of material as a whole. This book attempts such a treatment by surveying the general field of military occupational song and drawing on the legacy of a series of twentieth-century wars. A broad, representative selection of excerpts has been made from the total volume of material potentially available. Readers wanting to know more about particular texts should consult any published sources it has been possible to cite after each title. The field of military song is enormous, and it has not been possible to provide more than a representative sample of the ordinary soldier's repertoire. The output of wartime popular music is even greater, and only some of its main outlines have been indicated here. However, the texts of a number of military songs have been reproduced in full, either because they hold some particular interest or are not easily obtainable elsewhere. Whatever information it has been possible to compile about tunes and specific sources has been cited with each song title or is discussed in notes to each chapter. Music for a few tunes that are not well known, or have not (as far as the author is aware) been published elsewhere, has been included. An asterisk after the name of an author or a performer in a citation indicates that music is included with the text of a song, or exists in recorded form.

The work contains a combination of personal narrative and anecdote as well as field data, interviews with survivors, letters, diaries, tape recordings, folklore and historical narrative. Because some of this material has dimensions that transcend time as well as geographic space, the content ranges from World War 1 to Vietnam and makes use of comparative material from U.S., British Commonwealth and other sources.

Illustrations have been obtained from the National Archives in Washington, D.C., the Department of Defense Still Media Records Center in Washington, D.C. (official U.S. Army photos), the Library of Congress, the Turnbull Library of New Zealand and the author's own photographic collection.

In spite of every effort, it has proved impossible to establish the original sources of many of the traditional compositions cited here. Should a composer have been inadvertently overlooked, the author apologizes and would be glad to make proper attribution in any future edition of the work.

Many people have helped in this project either as informants or as consultants. In New Zealand, B. F. ("Mick") Shepherd of Auckland, Peter Ferguson of Gisborne, Sergeant Mike Subritzky of the Royal New Zealand Artillery Regiment and R. G. Webber, a former editor of *NZEF Times* (a World War 2 New Zealand Army newspaper), provided help and encouragement. Richard Bialostocki and Herman Gieck, both of Wellington, assisted with the translation of Polish and German songs.

In the United States, the staff of the Hoover Institution at Stanford, California, the staff of the Music Faculty Library at UCLA, Los Angeles, and the librarians of the folksong archives at the University of Western Kentucky at Bowling Green, Kentucky; the University of Indiana at Bloomington, Indiana; and the University of California at Berkeley have given assistance with inquiries. So, too, have Andy Bergman of Fort Defiance, Virginia, an expert on the popular music of World War 2, and Dr. Charles W. Getz of Hillsborough, California, a former USAF pilot and an authority on aviators' songs and traditions. The writer is indebted to Frank K. Lorenz, curator of Special Collections in the Hamilton College library, New York State, as well as to the staff of the National Museum of American History and in particular to Dr. Harold H. Langley, curator of Naval History.

The support of Victoria University of Wellington, New Zealand, with grants of leave and financial assistance at various times has also been helpful. However, without the enthusiasm and generosity of Professor Lydia Fish of the Anthropology Department, State University College at Buffalo, New York, as well as other members of the New York Folklore Society, this enterprise would never have been completed.

Some of the ideas developed in this book, especially those concerned with the concepts of power and powerlessness, were originally published in *New York Folklore*, Vol. XI, Nos. 1–4, 1985. The author is also indebted to Saul Broudy, a folksinger and musician from Philadelphia, for permission to cite his pioneering M.A. thesis, "G.I. Folklore in Vietnam" (1969).

Dark
Laughter

Introduction

Popular culture is important in wartime. It asserts the values of patriotism and nationhood, it expresses people's emotional feelings and it helps them adapt to new roles and situations. Under the mobilizing banners of "the war effort," it enthuses the civilian labor force with a sense of individual worth and national urgency that is especially valuable when it is directed into unfamiliar and sometimes uncongenial and industrial tasks. It also allocates status to those called upon to help with patriotic fund raising, or with the entertainment and welfare of troops. In this way, ordinary citizens as well as celebrities can experience the integratory gratifications of community service. Those most in need of reassurance are draftees who have to adapt to communal arrangements for sleeping, eating, training, recreation and amusement as well as having to accept the disquieting possibilities of physical combat and injury or even loss of life.

When large numbers of civilians are inducted into military service, their compliance is usually obtainable by means of indoctrination and discipline. However, this compliance is likely to be reinforced in wartime by a homeland production of patriotic sentiment and exhortation that is dedicated to the nation's cause and depicts war as a heroic crusade. Under the romantic justification of service for their country, twentieth-century campaigners have been expected to put up with reduced pay, indifferent food, sequestration in substandard accommodations, monotony, boredom, hardship and personal danger. To nudge them into cheerful acceptance of such inconveniences and to convert reluctant civilians into cooperative and even enthusiastic warriors requires a considerable effort in socialization.

The popular culture is ambivalent about this process. While it supports the current social order, it also expresses and integrates what have been termed "disturbing experiences that are not supposed to be there" (Fluck 1987). In wartime, these emerge as contradictions between the ideological hyperbole of popular culture content and the daily actualities experienced by its consumers. To a wife or mother, it may be the difference between the lofty rhetoric of sacrifice and the sorrowful loss or injury of a loved one. To a soldier, it is the disparity between the ideal and the actual, measurable in the contrast between patriotic fervor and battlefield realities. It may also be seen as an antithesis between the romantic fantasies of popular music, film and literature and the disturbing logic of casualty rates and combat stress disorders. Or it may emerge in the conflict between officially sponsored values of loyalty, honor, manliness, courage, heroism, regimental pride, achievement of the mission and the normal, personal desire for self-preservation and survival.

This treatment of war as popular culture uses services songs, folklore and popular music as a leitmotif to explore some of the cultural relationships between military life and society. Its content is largely restricted to Anglo-American sources because England, the British Commonwealth and the United States have a democratic heritage of personal liberty of expression, they share a voluminous interchange of popular music and entertainment and they possess many elements of a common Anglo-American folklore, particularly in the area of military occupational song. Patriotic, nostalgic and nationalistic images abound in the popular lyrics of most other nation-states, but to include them all is beyond the scope of the present work.

This work surveys the general field of military occupational song in order to illustrate some of the typical ways that popular culture deals with the emotional and social crises of wartime by providing soldiers with a comprehensive repertoire of integrative precepts which present their new occupations as an extension of homeland experience and a transplantation of some of its social arrangements.

The occupational songs of the services are only one element of wartime popular culture. Even more widely familiar are the popular songs of the nation, which are profusely amplified through the mass media for the general entertainment of the entire population, both services people and civilians. The wartime output of the mass media is a cultural production that defines patriotic goals and expresses the hopes, sentiments, emotional excitements and social concerns of the nation. Consequently, wartime popular music can be thought of as popular culture in its broadest sense, incorporating both the output of the commercial mass communications industries and the resources of folk culture in the form of occupational songs and narratives circulating among the military. In this way, the ordinary person in uniform is exposed to the typical sounds and images of the homeland as well as a great variety of musical parodies, burlesques, satires and other compositions of the kind that circulate informally.

Popular culture and folklore are interdependent. As part of a matrix of expressive activity and meaning in the lives of the rank and file, they mediate between discrepancies and help to integrate the individual into the framework of military life. Occupational song is one of the most powerful forms of industrial folklife. It proliferates in the wartime military services as a counterpoint to the content of popular music in what has been described by Narváez and Laba (1985:7) as a "folklore-popular culture continuum." The songs of the rank and file are especially important in this relationship because they are an outlet for grumbling, discontent, fear, satire, derision and the expression of other sentiments that may be informally tolerated but have no officially approved voice.

Modern Western armies devote extensive resources to the social welfare and entertainment of their troops and for this purpose adopt whole segments of popular culture. Although warfare is becoming increasingly mechanized and technology-dominant, masses of unskilled labor in the form of infantry are still required to occupy ground and to engage in physical combat. However, much of the ordinary soldier's time is spent in camps, bivouacs, supply bases and support organizations in the rear, handling stores, doing repetitive drills, exercising with weapons and equipment and carrying out routine maintenance and training. The amount of time actually devoted to aggressive action against tangible enemies may be comparatively brief. Apart from such interludes, the rest of the soldier's life is often a desert of discomfort and drudgery attending to barracks chores and exercising with weapons and equipment either in some base training establishment, some remote post or encampment or on some battlefield where most of the amenities and amusements of normal life are lacking.

An example of this spartan deprivation was evident in the television coverage of the Gulf War with its scenes of troops and armor deployed in desert landscapes of stark emptiness. The popular culture reacted with speedy patriotic fervor. Lee Greenwood, a country music star, wrote a special lyric, "You're the Great Defenders of the U.S.A." In a television interview he explained that it was intended to give the guys and gals in uniform a song "that would really address who they are and what they do for the country." His rendering of the familiar "God Bless America" got an airing on the Desert Radio Network, while Bette Midler's "Wind Beneath My Wings" received a lot of airplay at home. It was mixed with a track of a small boy reading a letter to his daddy in the desert and telling him he thought he was a hero. Against such impeccable sentiment, another lyric, "Give Peace a Chance," was less impressive. As for the troops, they composed a parody of a contemporary pop lyric sung by Milli Vanilli entitled "Blame it on the Rain." This song emerged in street rap style as "Gotta blame it on something . . . blame it on Hussein."

Many of the operational theaters of World War 1 and 2 were equally bleak frontiers with very few women and few civilized graces. Much of the time of their occupants was directed to the care and operation of the machinery with which modern armies are equipped. In that sense, warfare is a triumph of the techniques of mass production, with the soldier as a machine-tending, expendable unit of raw material. Consequently, being a soldier is rather like being detained in some dangerous industry from which the labor force cannot take a therapeutic holiday when it pleases or cannot obtain a transfer to some less threatening occupation. The military fondness for standardization and routine, and its attempts to convert the soldier to the status of obedient robot are, of course, characteristic of modern mass production methods. Therefore, it is not surprising that military "workers" have problems of boredom, fatigue and homesickness and are sometimes given to grumbling, malingering, absenteeism and various kinds of deviancy.

To reduce the frequency of such disorders, wartime military commands, at least in Western armies, have found it convenient to maintain controlled linkages with the homeland by means of a morale-supporting program of comforts and diversions. These feature soldiers' letters and mail services that are important as a lifeline between the battlefield and the homeland. Barrett-Litoff and Smith (1990:39), in their study of mail and its contribution to morale in World War 2, claim that it was what, in almost unimaginable quantities, "held American dreams together in the time of separation and great trial." Not only letters but also parcels of comforts and favorite foodstuffs could be sent to the front.

Other important sources of welfare are religious counseling, telephone services, access to services canteens and organizations like the PX, the YMCA, the Red Cross and the USO. In addition, there are sports programs, services newspapers, radio and television programs, cassette tapes and videotapes that feature popular music and entertainers. These sources are augmented by the screening of films and the scheduling of field visits by concert parties and musical performers. This whole array of comforts and diversions amounts to a selective, export montage of the homeland popular culture using familiar distractions and facilities that are intended to fill in the soldier's free time and impart to military life a veneer of reassuring, domestic normality.

Using techniques of mass communication and persuasion, warfare can be sold to its nation-state consumers just as one can market any film, cosmetic, detergent, political movement or politician. Wartime popular cultures specialize in an enthusiastic industry of mass entertainment and propaganda that exploits every possible sentiment from nostalgic love of country to the platitudes of nationalism and whatever collective efforts might be made to mobilize resources for the war effort. The social function of this cultural production is to integrate the nation and reinforce its solidarity by presenting both military and industrial service as a crusading, patriotic duty to be performed with enthusiastic dedication.

The patriotic songs of World War 1 attempted to satisfy this function with the symbolism of God, King, Country, national flags and national heroes. This iconography was accompanied by the strident assertions of Tin Pan Alley songwriters that "The Ocean Shall be Free," "Uncle Sam Will Help You Win the War," "We're Going Through to Berlin," "We are Going to Whip the Kaiser," "We Shall Never Surrender Old Glory," and "Just Like Washington Crossed the Delaware, General Pershing Will Cross the Rhine." "America First," a 1916 lyric, displayed a portrait of George Washington on the sheet music cover, and declared that the star spangled banner would always be defended and that "America First" would be the nation's battle cry.

The music industry also promoted an alternative view of the war as an opportunity for adventurous excitement implicit in such entertainments as George M. Cohan's smash hit "Over There" and the big hit of *The Passing Show of 1917*—"Goodbye Broadway, Hello France." The war's potentialities as a subject for romantic, sentimental indulgence were typified in songs like "The Rose of No Man's Land" (a metaphor for the Red Cross nurse) and "Your Lips Are No Man's Land But Mine," a declaration by the departing warrior as he headed off to deal with "Old Kaiser Bill."

The American Expeditionary Force's commitment was treated as a comedy of manners in songs like the spirited "How 'Ya Gonna Keep 'Em Down on the Farm (After They've Seen Paree)" and the suggestive "When Yankee Doodle Learns to Parlez Vous Français," and in Irving Berlin's racy "Oh How I Hate to Get Up in the Morning," an enduring hit that was featured in *Yip, Yip, Yaphank*, the stage show he wrote and appeared in. The song was so successful that Berlin used it again in 1942 in a Broadway musical called *This Is the Army*, which went on tour until 1945 and was also made into a movie. Perhaps the height of idiocy in the comedy of manners genre was reached in a 1918 number entitled "Come on Papa" in which an enticing Parisienne picks up American soldiers in her motor car and kisses them with frequent repetitions of "Oo-la-la!"

Songs that urged civilian males to join up and do their bit for King and Country (in the case of England) or for Nation and Flag (in the case of the United States) were plentiful in World War 1. One of the most famous was a plangent 1914 lyric entitled "Your King and Country Want You." Subtitled "a woman's recruiting song," this slow march gravely informed potential warriors of their personal importance to the nation and promised them gratitude and kisses when they returned from its service. However, "America Here's My Boy" took a much more militant approach to recruitment. In this song a grimly determined mother said she had raised her only son for America and if she had another, he too would march beside his brother.

Another patriotic offering, entitled "If I Had a Son for Each Star in Old Glory," was described by its publishers, Leo Feist Inc., as "doing its bit by helping recruit regiments for Uncle Sam." But there was a radically alternative view of the responsibilities of motherhood. It was voiced in "I Didn't Raise My Boy to Be a Soldier" (subtitled "A Mother's Plea for Peace, respectfully dedicated to every Mother—everywhere"). This 1915 composition warned prophetically of 10 million soldiers going to the war and protested that warfare would cease if other mothers made the same pacifistic declaration as she had.

The antithesis of the sacrificial heroics of militant motherhood could also be heard among the resources of folklore. "That Bloody War" began as a burlesque of the sabre-rattling excitements that accompanied the Spanish-American War. It used a variant of the tune of "The Battleship Maine." In its World War 1 version (Indiana), the reluctant anti-hero is "a harmless country hick a'workin' on a farm" until the sheriff calls to notify him that Uncle Sam needs his services. After a series of absurd misadventures, he reaches the trenches where he is frightened by a bomb explosion, whereupon he throws down his gun and runs away.

> The Captain asked me why I ran,
> I said the reason why,
> The only reason that I ran
> Was 'cos I couldn't fly!
> Bloody war! Oh, bloody war!
>
> I ran all over Europe
> A'fightin' for my life
> And before I go to war again
> I'll send my darlin' wife!
> Bloody war! Oh, bloody war!

Several popular songs of World War 1 expose an underlying discrepancy between conventional patriotic banalities about the war and the bitter actualities encountered at the front. These are some of the great song hits of the period. "Keep the Home Fires Burning," "It's a Long Way to Tipperary" and "There's a Long, Long Trail" have a simple expressive power as statements of nostalgic endurance, with an underlying, mournful awareness of what in fact was happening in the trenches. Soldiers could sing them on the march to any appropriate tempo, and they could take on an almost hymnlike, inspirational quality. "There's a Long, Long Trail" imagines a land of dreams and a long night of waiting until these dreams are realized. Brophy and Partridge (1965:216) note that the song had the rhythm of the daily routines of the war and its huge, complicated tasks for which no end was in sight. Its consciousness of separation from loved ones could easily lead to the secret speculation that it might be forever.

Perhaps such fantasies about a land of dreams with long nights and winding trails were a displacement of acute anxieties and fears by people trapped in the labyrinth of steel and the interminable maze of trenches in the battlefields of France. They are examples of the oblique emergence of disquieting concerns about experiences "that are not supposed to be there" in the text of a popular song that achieved an emotional universality through two world wars. A more brutal statement of the actual fate of many warriors could only be directly expressed in folksong. Death is a taboo subject in popular song and is reverently distanced in the appropriate consecration of religious, commemorative and funeral observances. However, its grinning presence was recognized overtly in World War 1 soldiers' songs like "The Hearse Song" ("The worms crawl in and the worms crawl out, they'll crawl all over your chin and your mouth") and "When the Guns Are Rolling Yonder" ("You'll be lying in the rain with the shrapnel in your brain and you'll never see your sweetheart any more"). The folksong component of the comprehensive envelope of popular culture can be used to discuss not only death, but also other subjects not officially encouraged.[1]

The popular songs of World War 2 emphasized the ideal of sacrifice for the common cause and singled out targets like Hitler, "The Fascist beasts," the Nazis and "the dirty little Jap," treating them sometimes as stereotypes of menacing evil and sometimes as ludicrous caricatures. On the whole, however, they relied less on jingoism and the deity and more on the patriotic values of nationhood in songs like "God Bless America," "There'll Always Be an England" and "This Is Worth Fighting For." Timely incident inspired "Remember Pearl Harbor," while Frank Loesser's "Praise the Lord and Pass the Ammunition" with its dirgelike tune and its combination of faith and militancy appealed to the post–1941 apprehensions of its American audience. Simple nostalgia inspired "Till the Lights of London Shine Again," "The White Cliffs of Dover," "When They Sound the Last All Clear," "I'll Be Seeing You," "You'll Never Know Just How Much I Love You," "We'll Meet Again" and "When the Lights Go on Again."

Songwriters of World War 2 continued to treat the services as a location for glamorous sexual adventure in numbers like "My USO Dreamgirl," "The Red Cross Girl of the U.S.A.," "Madamoiselle from Normandy," "Sweetheart of the Infantry" and "I'm Dreaming of a Military Wedding."

The comedy of manners produced some frantic trivia in the idiotic "Run, Rabbit, Run," the absurd "Mairzy Doats," the ridiculous "Kiss Me Goodnight Sergeant Major," the frivolous "Nursie! Nursie!" the inane "Even Hitler Had a Mother," the ludicrous "We're Going to Hang out the Washing on the Siegfried Line" along with labored attempts at wit in "I'm a G.I. Cowboy," "The Honey Bucket Train to Tokyo," "My Yankee Doodle Boy Can Bet on Me," "Our Hootin', Tootin', Shootin', Yankee Boys," "Twinkle, Twinkle Little Spar," "Der Führer's Face" and "Goodbye Mamma I'm off to Yokohama."

Hits like "Don't Sit Under the Apple Tree," "Wonder When My Baby's Coming Home," "They're Either Too Young or Too Old" and "No Love, No Nothing" assumed that the male warrior would enjoy the sexual admiration and devotion of all right-minded, patriotic females, though an occasional number like "Sergeant Sally Is Coming Home on Leave" and "The WAC in Back of You" signaled the beginning of an era of changing rules for women. On the home front the importance of the female industrial worker was recognized in songs like "Zelda the Welder," "Rosy the Riveter" and "Beltline Girl" who steps into a limited tenure of the assembly line to replace "Joe" who has gone to the fighting front. She declares dutifully that the faster the beltline girls work, the sooner "our boys" return.

Such songs had an obvious didactic purpose in mobilizing the civilian workforce and giving it a sense of self-worth and patriotic dedication. However, they seldom reached the pitch of hysterical excitement attained in totalitarian Germany where official propaganda made intensive use of all mass media, particularly radio, as well as mass meetings and other Nazi party and state-sponsored activities. Group singing was encouraged, and soldiers were expected to learn a repertoire of marching songs and traditional items that they could perform on command. Music was an important element in National Socialism, which had a large accompaniment of fighting songs about the *Sturmabteilung* as well as a plethora of adulatory compositions about Adolf Hitler (Meyer 1977).

The German music industry also produced a great many moralebuilding lyrics in World War 2. Some of them became popular favorites. An example was "Es geht alles Vorüber," a catchy pop number that was often played and sung as a morale booster, rather like the British "Things Are Getting Better All the Time."

> All our troubles are over
> They are fading away
> Like the snow in December
> And the sunshine in May. (Author's translation)

The BBC in its propaganda broadcasts to Nazi Germany devised a topical parody of this song that emphasized food shortages, including a lack of Schnapps. German troops, hearing this parody, came up with their own subversive version to this effect.

> It's all passing over,
> We've had the lot;
> The Schnapps available last December
> We'll be scratching for in May;
> First falls the Leader
> And then the Party. (Author's translation)

After the German invasion of the Soviet Union, the Soviet propaganda machine circulated frantic patriotic appeals to resist the invader and defend "Mother Russia." A typical example of this rhetoric was "Holy War," widely used as an official marching song.

> Awake great country!
> Awake for a great war!
> Awake for a final fight
> With Fascist power.
> Against that damned movement
> Our fury burns!
> The war is on now! (Author's translation)

Popular entertainment in the Soviet Union was mobilized for patriotic purposes by a Ministry of Culture, which arranged visits to the front by concert parties and entertainers. One of the most celebrated of these artists was Klavdya Shulzhenko, a director and soloist with the famous Leningrad Ensemble. The Ensemble consisted of a small orchestra and a group of singers who gave concerts close to the frontline as well as in armament factories and hospitals. Shulzhenko had a voice of haunting lyric power, but the items the troops asked her to sing were more likely to be nostalgic reminders of home, or familiar love songs, rather than the patriotic fulminations of Soviet bureaucracy.

A favorite item was "The Soldiers' Waltz" ("It's a long time since I've seen my loved one; we are so far from our homeland"). Another was "Kubanka" (a particular kind of Cossack fur cap).

> Quiet evening beyond the Volga,
> The sunset like a dying fire;
> My dearest I would love to speak
> To you about my love;
> I am talking to you now,
> But I have different thoughts on my mind;
> Maybe tomorrow in the blue morning
> I will ride the wild horse. Etc. (Author's translation)

Well-known love songs like "My Dearest Don't Cry, There is No Need To," "The Dark Night" and "Are You Waiting Elizabeth?" appealed to the feelings of those caught up in gigantic turmoil.

> Are you waiting Elizabeth
> For a greeting from your lover?
> You don't sleep till the sunrise,
> And you are sad about me;
> But when you are worried and yearning,
> Don't stand on the threshold looking anxiously,
> I'll come back when the snow melts. Etc. (Author's translation)

Perhaps one of the most poignant songs of World War 2 was least concerned with the heroics of Soviet ideology. This was "In the Dugout." The singer is sitting in a dugout by a small fire. Its embers are burning like tears, and an accordion is singing of his lover's eyes and smile. She is far away and very hard to reach, "but death is only four steps away."

Patriotic purpose and the imperatives of national mobilization may have great urgency for political regimes, but audience responses are the ultimate test of a song's success, whether it is being pushed by the propaganda agencies of a totalitarian state or whether it is being aggressively marketed in a democracy. This is why attempts by the U.S. music industry to find a "correct" formula for World War 2 songs were unsuccessful. The U.S. Office of War Information and the American Theater Wing Committee considered the possibilities of popular music as military propaganda, but it was soon found that there was no payoff in high purpose or patriotic intent. A song had to be accepted by the mass audience for its qualities as entertainment. According to *Variety*

Nobody has yet been able to lead the nation to the musical trough and making 'em drink. You can pound at them through all manner of high-powered song plugging and exploitation, but what they'll accept one never knows until the copies move off the racks.[2]

The attempt to find ideologically "correct" songs for the services proved equally abortive.

Sometimes we vote for certain "properly inspirational" tunes but even the soldiers themselves go for the sentimental oldies, again proving the axiom that you can lead a song to the mike, but you can never make the public buy it.[3]

Soldiers in World War 2 not only were entertained by film, touring stage shows and concert parties, but they also generated their own music. Wherever the U.S. Army went, it had its own regimental jazz groups and instrumental combinations as well as military brass bands that could render marches and other popular compositions in a jazz idiom. Jazz was also played extensively by Armed Forces Radio stations. By such means it was exported on a global scale. Its enjoyment was enhanced by the contemporary craze for jitterbugging to the strains of "The Boogie Woogie Bugle Boy of Company B," "In the Mood," "Deep in the Heart of Texas," "Tiger Rag" and other song hits of the period.

The emotional gratifications of wartime popular music included not only the pleasures of sexual pursuit and the dance, but also the sentimental attractions of identification with the nation's cause and the enhancement of self-identity as a warrior, loved one, adventurous crusader, partaker of hospitality and beneficiary of the integrative rewards of fraternization in dance halls, bars, canteens, services clubs, posts and barracks.

The army also attempted to supply the troops with the means for self-entertainment in the form of complete shows that were packaged with musical arrangements and staging instructions and sent out to units in the field as "Hit-Kits." A typical Hit-Kit show contained a few comic songs with jokes about services haircuts, drill and discipline, some inspirational items like "Moving Along Together," "Man to Man" ("There's a pride inside you for the infantry"), "Ch'i Lai" (described as "the favorite marching song of the Chinese volunteers") and "Meadowland" (said to be "the favorite marching song of the Russian Army," though in fact, Soviet troops were more attracted to sentimental and romantic popular lyrics). There were sentimental tributes to the girl back home like "Shoo-Shoo Baby," "No Love, No Nothing" and "Wait for me Mary." Finally, the typical show concluded with "Soldiers of God," the official chaplain's march. The kits were issued monthly and often drew extensively on the words and music of current song hits. For instance, the April 1943 issue contained "Coming in on a Wing and a Prayer," "There's a Star Spangled Banner Waving Somewhere," "This Time," "I Just Kissed Your Picture Goodnight" and "Roll Out the Barrel."

Hit-Kits and similar recreational amenities in the U.S. Army in World War 2 were administered by the Special Services Division of the U.S. Army Service Forces. The Division published a *Soldier Shows Guide* for use by units in the field. It contained useful technical information about blackouts, staging, the writing of sketches, quizzes, parodies and other simple routines. A Writers' War Board had a committee on scripts for services shows which produced sketch books of suitable revue, vaudeville and comedy acts. For instance, its 1943 edition contained Abbott and Costello, Fred Allen, Burns and Allen, Charlie McCarthy and Fibber and Molly McGee scripts. There was sufficient talent in the ranks for the Special Services Division of the North African Theater of Operations to hold a songwriters' contest in July 1943. There were 199 entries. The winners were "For Evermore" by Fred Valdez, "Marching Along to Berlin" by Lyle Moraine, "The Dream that Jack Built" by Errol Anton and

"Love Isn't Censored" by Samuel Snead. The entries contained seventy-six love songs, twenty-eight army and drinking songs, eleven patriotic numbers and a variety of miscellaneous lyrics.

Other Special Services revues were "About Face" and "Pfc. Mary Brown" (a WAC musical). Troops that were not up to producing a full-scale stage show could always resort to the Division's *Ten-Minute Self-Instructor for the Tonette, Ocarina, Harmonica and Ukelele*, published in 1943. Or they could consult its *Pocket Guide for the U.S. Army Song Leader*. This was a thirty-six-page booklet which advised that "a singing army is a fighting army." It expounded the fundamental techniques of song-leading and amateur song-conducting. "A good song leader should be able to start people singing on almost any occasion and under almost any conditions or handicaps." It concluded with a list that ranged from inspirational items like "The Star Spangled Banner," "America" and "The Battle Hymn of the Republic" to marching songs ("Tipperary," "Pack Up Your Troubles," "The Caissons Go Rolling Along"), old favorites like "Home on the Range" and other "singable songs" from *The Army Songbook*, a publication issued by the U.S. War Department. In the Korean War, an *Armed Forces Song Folio* was issued monthly by the Departments of the Army, the Navy and the Air Force.

The increasingly mechanized and technology-dependent mass armies of the twentieth century have come to rely extensively on civilian-based organizations as a necessary humanizing source of spiritual as well as material well-being for the conscript soldier. A pioneering example of this development was the YMCA. This organization was founded in England in 1844 as an interdenominational and international movement that sought to help young people to accept the Christian faith and lead a Christian life. A worldwide network had been formed by the 1850s. World War 1 presented it with an unprecedented opportunity to proselytize. Both the British and the American YMCAs were active among the Allied forces, as were the Salvation Army, the Church Army and the Red Cross. Often in the towns and villages of France, the huts established by these organizations were the only places that were warm and dry, where books and magazines could be read, where a piano or a gramophone could be played, where writing materials were on hand and where a hot drink, doughnuts, sandwiches and even cakes could be obtained. The huts were sometimes tents, sometimes a shed in a village, perhaps a dugout or a disused barracks, or occasionally a large timber structure specially built for the purpose. It all depended on the ingenuity of fieldworkers.

The American YMCA requisitioned hotels in Paris and in the French Alps where soldiers could spend their leave and be encouraged to divert themselves from the temptations of drink and prostitution. With this in mind, the sponsors of the scheme recruited female as well as male staff because they thought "the presence of really good women alongside the men workers in YMCA huts was of the highest military, moral and social value" (Mayo 1931:19).

The American YMCA in World War 1 took on the enormous additional responsibility of running the American Expeditionary Force's Post Exchange Service (usually known as the PX). This was a kind of general store or canteen with about 10 million customers. The money for this enterprise originally came from the U.S. Army Department, and all the goods had to sell at factory cost. The more immediate needs of the troops were met by "rolling canteens" consisting of a motor lorry that carried a copper boiler, firewood, a supply of water for making coffee and whatever foodstuffs might be available. These goods were driven up to wherever troops were billeted or wherever they were in transit behind the lines. Many women distinguished themselves in this service. Some drove rolling canteens, and others ran canteens at field dressing stations and field hospitals where they often helped the army nursing services. A number of YMCA secretaries, both men and women, were wounded, shell-shocked, gassed, killed and also awarded decorations.

A YMCA entertainment department fielded a total of 35,000 volunteers to run movie shows, soldier shows and lectures as well as performances by stock companies throughout the areas occupied by the American Expeditionary Force (AEF). Evans and Harding (1921) describe how the first entertainers to appear among the troops in 1917 were C. E. Clifford Walker (a pianist and singer), Maletsky (a French musician with a troupe of performing rabbits) and Cobbina Johnson (a grand opera contralto). Many celebrities subsequently made the trip to France including Margaret Wilson, one of President Woodrow Wilson's daughters. An Over There Theatre League sent entertainment troupes to the front with names like "Some Pep," the "Y Minstrels," the "Electric Sparks," "Just Girls," "Magic, Melody and Music," the "Shamrock Show," the "Broadway Bunch" and the "Mayo Shock Unit." Jazz was being played by combinations like the "Scrap Iron Jazz Band," especially after the Armistice when the troops were waiting impatiently for transport home. Song leaders were also trained and sent overseas with supplies of songbooks and leaflets intended to get the troops singing popular refrains.

The American Red Cross in World War 1 had an even more massive and onerous responsibility to recruit and maintain its own corps of nurses while organizing, staffing and equipping ambulance units, hospitals and convalescent homes and supplying them from large depots of medical and surgical stores that it also administered. In addition to hospital care, it provided comforts, welfare and entertainments services on a large scale.

In its welfare work the American Red Cross cooperated broadly with the Salvation Army, the YMCA, the agencies of the National Jewish Welfare Board, the Knights of Columbus, the Society of Friends, the American Library Association and the War Camp Service. The work of these bodies was coordinated by a Commission on Camp Training Activities that concerned itself with recreational, educational and religious care for servicemen. The Red Cross operated hundreds of canteens for soldiers in the United States. It provided light meals for them on trains, and it gave emergency medical care for those in transit.

By the time the Armistice was signed in 1918, the Red Cross had twenty-one hospitals in France, twelve convalescent homes, nine infirmaries, ten dispensaries, a navy hospital, and a hospital for auxiliary army personnel and civilians doing quasimilitary duty. In addition, there were thirteen convalescent hospitals in England for American wounded (Hurd 1954:169). It ran a volunteer ambulance brigade in Italy and supplied many of the base hospitals used by the military in England and France. As well as theaters, restaurants and hostels, it operated 130 canteens.

The welfare activities of the American Red Cross were greatly expanded during World War 2. Its field directors set up canteens, and distributed coffee and doughnuts, comforts and supplies, especially to the sick and wounded. They provided recreation tents equipped with games, radio, recordings and magazines, and they also engaged in personal counseling.

The directors could call on a home service program that used volunteers in the homeland. On behalf of servicemen, they could obtain information about insurance and benefits and could get reports about dependents' legal or business affairs. They could borrow money to meet people's personal emergencies, and they could arrange counseling for personal problems. This welfare work was no minor activity: in 1944 they made emergency loans amounting to more than $18 million. According to *The American Red Cross with the Armed Forces* (1945), this assistance was often needed because troops were moving about so rapidly that sometimes the pay service could not keep up with them. The field directors had special access to the military communications system to help them with this work. Thus, in 1944 a total of 1,600 messages per day were being relayed between Red Cross workers overseas and those operating the home service. This extensive traffic was carried over military radio with reduced priority. It offered a speedy linkage between the field and the homeland without formally involving military officials. About 3 million servicemen and their families received assistance from this service in 1944.

The American Red Cross also ran rehabilitation programs for veterans in military hospitals where, in 1945, it had about 3,000 social and recreational staff on duty. Mobile hospital units on trains and ships carried

Red Cross workers, while in domestic hospitals the Red Cross staff was supported by local members of the Hospital and Recreation Corps known as "Grey Ladies." These ladies did shopping errands for the bedridden, wrote letters for the disabled, talked to the lonely and distributed comforts.

In cooperation with the U.S. Army's Special Service officers and the U.S. Navy's Welfare officers, the Red Cross field directors and recreation workers helped arrange for movies, stage shows, bridge and checkers tournaments, debates, golf matches, dances, amateur talent nights, musical programs and community entertainments. For instance, a Red Cross show called *On Stage* consisting of musical items and sketches was available for use wherever U.S. troops were stationed. In 1944 patients in 407 army and navy hospitals saw 220,000 showings of movies in hospital wards that relied on Red Cross equipment. In addition, the Red Cross screened movies in hospital auditoriums and recreation centers.[4]

Overseas, a network of Red Cross clubs was available for the use of the armed forces. By 1945, a total of 740 clubs had been established in leave centers. Most of them had a dining room, a lounge with newspapers, books and writing materials, a recreation room with a piano, card tables, ping pong tables, an information desk, a laundry and pressing service, a sewing and mending service, money-changing facilities, a snack bar, a first-aid station and sleeping accommodations. One club in London could feed 2,000 at a sitting and could sleep 700 a night. The monthly attendance at dances, movies and concerts at Red Cross clubs in England before D-Day averaged about 300,000. In all of them, a visitor could get American coffee and hear the voice of at least one of the 2,000 Red Cross women serving abroad.

Some Red Cross field canteens were staffed entirely by women. For instance, three women worked shifts to maintain a twenty-four-hour service at a roadside stand in southern France in 1944 called "The Truckers' Rest" for drivers hauling supplies to the front. On the Fifth Army front in Italy, the Red Cross coffee and doughnut stand on Route 65 turned out an average of 10,000 doughnuts daily. In December 1944 this establishment was being run by three Red Cross workers with eight Italian staff.

In World War 2 the U.S. Army brought enormous resources to bear on the general problem of welfare. Its Army Service Forces Division directed programs of morale-building activity that included athletics, entertainment, recreation and welfare in any part of the globe where U.S. troops were active. At each camp, post or installation in the United States, a Personal Affairs officer was responsible for counseling troops needing advice about pay, insurance, dependents' allowances, furlough, legal aid, pensions, decorations and medals, rehabilitation and training for postwar employment, the G.I. Bill of Rights and any other problems.

The concept of interdenominational cooperation, successfully pioneered by the various welfare agencies in World War 1, was the means for a remarkable development in the entertainment and hospitality field in World War 2. The United Service Organizations (USO) was formed in Washington, D.C., in 1941 by six national agencies: the International Committee of the YMCA, the National Board of the YWCA, the National Catholic Community Service, the National Jewish Welfare Board, the Salvation Army and the National Travellers' Aid Association of America. It was financed by voluntary contributions, but its work was under the general direction of a joint Army and Navy Committee on Welfare and Recreation. President Roosevelt officially asked the USO to undertake a program of morale, recreation and religious work for men in the services and for people in defense industries.

Later, a branch known as USO Camp Shows was formed. Big-name stars were asked to give their services free, while less affluent performers were paid from publicly subscribed USO funds. During the next three years, about 3,500 performers made over 35,000 personal appearances. Entertainment circuits were created among army posts, naval stations and military hospitals in the United States, while a "foxhole circuit" took stars like Joe E. Brown, Bob Hope, Laurel and Hardy, Jack Benny, Bing Crosby, Ann Sheridan, Paulette Goddard, Gary Cooper, Carole Landis, Frances Langford, Kay Francis, Al Jolson, Ray Milland, Ray Bolger, Larry Adler, Dinah Shore, Fred Astaire and Humphrey Bogart on overseas tours.

The American Theater Wing War Service Organization ran the famous Stage Door Canteen in New York and also sent professional show troupes out to factories to entertain war workers. In 1943 a group called "Lunchtime Follies" was doing chorus-line routines and singing "Put Another Nail in Hitler's Coffin" along with a Harold Rome follies lyric, "The Lady's on the Job," which announced that Uncle Sam had acquired a niece with elbow grease.

The group also performed a Kurt Weill number called "Inventory" which perfectly caught the patriotic emphasis on wartime production-line skills with its message of thousands of ships, subs and planes made by ordinary workers involved in complex sequences of assembly-line operations.

Similarly, the Hollywood Writers' Mobilization, in cooperation with the American Theater Wing, had eight troupes entertaining around Western industrial plants. The "Fliegelholm Welding School" with Zelda the Welder used boogie rhythms to publicize women's roles in war work. "You Look Better to Me Now" was one of the lyrics that signaled a wartime sexual revolution by romanticizing the woman on the assembly line who, at least for the purposes of the war effort, was said to be more alluring in her overalls than in a party gown.

Apart from its expansive effects on the wartime economy, World War 2 provided the U.S. film industry with adventurous and patriotic subjects for the production of a flood of morale-building war movies. These were aimed primarily at the civilian box office, but in 1942 the industry began supplying prints of all Hollywood films free of charge to services personnel in combat areas, hospitals and isolated posts overseas.

The tradition of patriotic commitment by the USO was continued in the Korean conflict and in the Vietnam War. By the 1990s the USO was maintaining about 100 centers around the world and running canteens and entertainment programs wherever U.S. forces might be located. For instance, Bob Hope gave USO-sponsored performances aboard ships of the Sixth Fleet at Christmas 1983 when it was supporting a Marine Corps force in Beirut. For the eighty-year-old Hope it was his thirty-first trip abroad as a services entertainer. In 1987 he took a USO Christmas show to the Persian Gulf where U.S. forces were stationed.

U.S. troops also keep in touch with the popular culture of the homeland through the Armed Services Radio and Television Network. This began as a radio service in Alaska in 1941 when soldiers on Kodiak Island improvised a low-power broadcasting transmission of recordings, news and locally generated programs. By 1942 the War Department had authorized the production of special radio programs for a full-time service. At the peak of World War 2, about 21,000 transcriptions per week were being sent overseas for broadcast to the troops in Europe, Asia, Alaska and the South Pacific. During the decades that followed, radio networks were maintained as part of a global communications system that extended over all the territories where U.S. troops were deployed. It emerged that there was also a foreign civilian audience of some millions for its output, partly because of the up-to-date, popular music it carried and also because listening to it was a convenient way to improve one's English. The service also extended into television as this technology developed.

The American nation at war not only supplies its troops with many facilities of life available in the homeland, but it also enters with enthusiastic energy into a gigantic industry of support for the common cause. This ranges from subscribing to war loans and patriotic appeals, taking part in concerts and fund-raising efforts, and sharing in the collective gratifications of the assembly line, the production team or the project staff mobilized for victory, to direct, personal involvement with troops' entertainment and welfare services. The sense of personal identification with military operations has been further extended by the advent of television. The ordinary citizen can now follow the fortunes of U.S. troops abroad in the kind of profuse visual detail with which both the Vietnam War and the Gulf conflict were covered. An indication of the expressive strength of the emotional linkages that accompany this enhanced scrutiny of events could be seen in the patriotic display of flags on people's houses during the Gulf War and in the custom of displaying yellow ribbons that signified the warrior's absence on Gulf operations and the dedication of those awaiting his or her return.[5]

The military services are a familiar and often prominent part of the popular culture of most nations, especially in the field of music. Wartime gives popular music an extra urgency and currency. For example, the American Civil War inspired a kind of popular musical eruption, visible today in a large, published repository of melodies, comic songs, marches, anthems, laments, sentimental and nostalgic airs as well as inspirational and patriotic appeals by both sides to the conflict. Much of this music dealt in a conventional, banner-we-love, dear-native-land, up-and-at-them, victory-or-death hyperbole that has as much relationship to the savage realities of war as the contemporary soap opera "M*A*S*H" has to the real horrors of a surgical ward in a field hospital on any modern battlefield, or as the comic absurdities of "Hogan's Heroes" (a puerile television comedy series about life in a German World War 2 prison camp) had to the wretched existence of the actual occupants of such places.

A few Civil War songs poked fun at being drafted and grumbled about headquarters getting the best food, at being kept on short rations, going barefoot and putting up with bugs and other hardships, but the best of them had a zestful energy and a lyric quality that have ensured their survival at the traditional center of American indigenous popular music. Songs and anthems like "The Battle Hymn of the Republic," "John Brown's Body," "Dixie," "The Battle Cry of Freedom," "Tramp, Tramp, Tramp, the Boys Are Marching," "When Johnny Comes Marching Home" and "Marching Through Georgia" had a poignant intensity that marked a formative stage in the history of the nation.

The Spanish-American War of 1898 produced another crop of sentimental airs like "Tell Mother Goodbye for Me," "My Sweetheart in Brown and Blue" and "Mother Dear My Country Calls Me." This was accompanied by an outburst of jingoistic sentiment in songs like "Wrap the Flag Around Me When I'm Dead," "Cuba Shall be Free," "Our Gallant Yankee Tars," "The Roughriders' Charge Song," "Uncle Sam" and a whole broadside of compositions about the sinking of the battleship *Maine*. But nothing possessed the distinction and permanence of the best of the Civil War songs.

The further growth of a nationalistic musical tradition in the nineteenth century owed more to composers and musicians like John Philip Sousa who in 1897 wrote "The Stars and Stripes Forever." As director of the United States Marine Band, and later of his own touring organization, Sousa composed a series of famous marches and operas, made

Bob Hope and Reita Faria (Miss World) on stage at the South Beach Amphitheater, Cam Ranh Bay, South Vietnam, 21 December 1966. *(U.S. Army)*

The cast of French performers at a show for Allied troops in North Africa, January 1943. *(National Archives)*

Base hospital banquet and dance at Camp Devens, Ayer, Massachusetts, November 1918. *(National Archives)*

John McCormack, the famous Irish tenor, singing for soldiers convalescing from wounds while cruising on Long Island Sound, October 1918. *(National Archives)*

Cathy O'Connor, a Red Cross worker in South Vietnam, distributing writing materials and paperbacks to troopers of the 173rd Airborne Brigade in a forward area, February 1966. *(U.S. Army)*

The American Red Cross doughnut factory at Le Mans, in France, 1918. Some 30,000 doughnuts per day were made here. *(National Archives)*

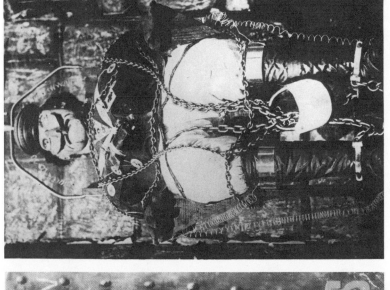

Left: A World War 2 postcard issued by the U.S. Treasury Department War Savings staff. *Right*: In World War 1 the citizens of Vallejo, California, kept an effigy of the Kaiser "on his rightful throne"—the electric chair—to remind them of their patriotic obligations. *(National Archives)*

The Garfield High School band wearing carnival masks and marching in a parade in Downtown Hollywood, 1989. (*Cleveland Collection*)

G.I.s and French civilians fraternizing in Le Mans, France, August 1944. *(National Archives)*

An American Red Cross canteen at Issoudon, France, 5 February 1919. *(National Archives)*

New Zealand Artillerymen "at work" in a World War 1 ammunition dump in France. (*The* Auckland Weekly News, *New Zealand, 30 November 1916. Courtesy of* The New Zealand Herald.)

German prisoners of war in a state of robot-like submission after their capture on the Somme in 1916. (*The* Auckland Weekly News, *New Zealand, 19 October 1916. Courtesy of* The New Zealand Herald.)

band arrangements of many national and patriotic anthems and gave over 10,000 concerts in the United States and abroad (Newsom 1983).

Sousa was an impresario who excelled at staging and dramatizing musical performances for large audiences. This element of showmanship is another prominent characteristic of American popular culture which through Broadway, Tin Pan Alley, Hollywood and television has been marketed to the entire globe. It combines showmanship, verbal wit, dramatic spectacle and popular music forms that have been enriched creatively by the unique ethnic composition of the American population. The universality of a popular style of musical performance that has been derived from military models is evident today in every American high school and college band that is uniformed as if for a Hollywood musical, plays on the march, performs parade ground maneuvers and appears as part of the local community on festive occasions. The onset of war reinforces these traditional martial elements in the popular culture and opens expanded fields for the participation of noncombatants and the expression of patriotic sentiment.

Parallel with the morale-building effusions of wartime however, there exists among the troops an entirely different and contradictory expressive tradition. This is located in the sphere of occupational song and military folklore. For instance, troops in World War 1 and World War 2 sang versions of "The Midnight Fusiliers," an eighteenth-century burlesque that ridicules military valor, and "I Don't Want to Be a Soldier," a composition that has been in circulation in the British Army since the Napoleonic Wars. (These and other examples are discussed in subsequent chapters.)

Such songs are oppositional to the dominant ideology of the popular culture, ridiculing the ideals of heroism and military propriety. Hundreds of them circulated in World War 2, illustrating the disparity between values that affirmed the righteousness and seriousness of the collective wartime effort and the nihilistic cynicism of its rank-and-file participants.

The main technique of composition used by unschooled wartime singers and musicians is parody, for the most part derived from the flood of popular music to which everyone in the armed services is exposed. A convenient World War 2 example of this technique was the wartime hit, "Bless 'Em All." It was copyrighted in 1940 and sung throughout World War 2 by Gracie Fields and other British entertainers. However, throughout the British and Commonwealth armies it was known as "Fuck 'Em All!," and the words of the troops' version were an expression of anger against the army and its authority system.

Popular culture contains the potential ingredients for expressing subversive and oppositional meanings, but it rarely ventures into the open statement of dissident, incongruent experience except in the case of the

Vietnam War (discussed in Chapter 7) where an oppositional homeland counterculture was able to penetrate the citadels of military control. The Vietnam experience apart, the main outlet for the overt and uninhibited expression of fears, criticism of, and opposition to, the prevailing ideology of both the military command and the homeland is usually located in the ranks in the form of occupational song, folklore, parodies, satires, ridicule and protest. This material is part of a total popular culture complex of expression that ranges from sentiments and exhortations that are ideologically compatible with official war aims, to feelings that are subversive of officially sponsored ideology. It is therefore a collective field of versatile consciousness that reassures and integrates, as it improvises responses to alarming or inconvenient experience and mocks at what it cannot alter or control. It offers the ordinary soldier entry into a psychological terrain of limitless expanse and imaginative reconciliation between the shining world of patriotic assertion and the disturbing realities of the battlefield. It mediates between "America Here's My Boy" and "Bloody War." It reconciles the imperatives of King and Country and Nation and Flag with the dolors of the long, long trail.

Such a resource can be drawn on, not just for passive entertainment and diversion, but for the management of personal crisis. It contains the psychological mechanisms of reassurance and integration that enable its possessors to express their emotions as they endure the consequences of social upheaval and separation from family, community and even society in the case of the Vietnam veterans. It enables people in the wartime military services to come to terms with their enforced tenure in institutions that by comparison with the freedom of democratic life are archaic and ultra-authoritative, focused as they are on the principle of unqualified obedience to the chain of command. Although their authority may be virtually omnipotent, they can still be mocked by the powerless who can draw on their store of occupational song and the content of the popular culture to ridicule their leaders and assert their personal dignity both in nostalgic lyrics and ribald parody "even at the cannon's mouth" (Cleveland 1985).

An important feature of military life is the way it favors the transmission of traditional lore from one generation to another and sometimes from one country to another. The major wars fought in the twentieth century have been a perfect milieu for the composition and transmission of songs, narratives and traditions by segregating vast numbers of young men and women in camps and barracks where, as part of the process of living communally, they have had to acquire new cultural perspectives in the groups in which they have found themselves arbitrarily assembled. Occupational song is important in this process of adjustment. It helps fill in time, and it provides flexible varieties of self-entertainment at locations where organized facilities are not always obtainable. It also heightens the sense of group identity and solidarity.

In this context, soldiers may have something in common with workers in accident-prone occupations like mining and firefighting. All are exposed to risk and must perform repetitive, often exhausting tasks in which skill is important and people have to rely on each other. Just as the songs of miners and other militant industrial workers chronicle their conflicts with management (as well as their struggles to survive in hazardous conditions), so a great number of combat soldiers' songs emphasize the dangers and hardships of life at the front, grumble about their superiors and wish they were safely at home or in the rear. The military equivalents of the industrial work song are the marching songs favored by all armies, as well as the cadence chants used by the U.S. armed services to coordinate the movements of bodies of troops by teaching them how to move in synchronization with repetitive chants and slogans that also help them to resist fatigue.

These songs may have some resemblance to the chants of prison laborers in the work gangs described by Jackson (1972:29–30). They helped pass the time, offered a partial outlet for tension, frustration and anger, and supplied a rhythm for the performance of manual labor. However, Jackson's comment that these prison songs were dying because of modernization and the use of machinery to perform tasks formerly done by manual labor is not applicable to all branches of the military. Although military organizations may fit Jackson's description of Texas prisons as an artificially maintained anachronism, and it is true that the military services are in general becoming more dependent on technology, they still have to rely on masses of relatively low-skilled human labor to perform the duties of infantry in time of war. They also persist with monotonous training routines like marching, drilling and fitness programs that are really varieties of physical work. Furthermore, technology itself is the substance of much occupational song, especially among air force pilots.

The occupational basis of services songs is also evident in their specialized vocabularies, their richly imaginative slang and the great number of compositions that deal with the technicalities of the work process, especially drilling, marching and the management of weaponry and equipment. Such a concern with the maintenance, servicing and operation of weapons and machinery might be expected since twentieth-century warfare is essentially an industrialized, mass production and mass consumption activity that is increasingly dependent on the disciplined performance of the work skills demanded by high technology. A glance at the navigational aids of any modern naval vessel, at the controls of any jet aircraft, at the range-finding equipment of any field artillery unit or at the signals system used by any modern combat formation indicates the extent to which mechanized warfare is enmeshed with technological resources that demand competent, disciplined performance by its users.

Some services songs acknowledge a central concern of twentieth-century life, which is more exercised by the problematic relationship between people and machines. In the officially endorsed occupational cultures of the military, the ideal condition is that of total integration. A classic example of a song that literally describes the machine and its operator as components of each other is "The Dying Aviator" or "The Handsome Young Airman."[6] The tune is "The Old Tarpaulin Jacket," a nineteenth-century ballad lamenting the death of a young seaman who on his deathbed asks his friends gathered around him to wrap him up in his old jacket.

Parodies of this song have proliferated in Australia. In "The Dying Stockman" (Paterson 1905:107–8), "a strapping young stockman lay dying/His saddle supporting his head." He asks his two mates to wrap him up with his stockwhip and blanket and to "bury me deep down below,/Where the dingoes and crows can't molest me/In the shade where the coolibahs grow." An index of Australian folksong (Edwards 1972a:21) cites "The Dying Bagman," "The Dying Fettler," "The Dying Shearer" and "The Dying Sleeper Cutter" as progeny of the stockman. Mountaineers and bush walkers in New Zealand in the 1970s sang about a starving young tramper who lay dying, "his rucksack supporting his head" (Cleveland Collection). Edwards (1973:32) gives three versions of "The Dying Harlot," an obscene parody in which "a dirty old harlot lay dying, a pisspot supporting her head," but the most enduring and widely known of this catalogue of mortality is "The Dying Aviator." It originated in World War 1 and was still being sung in World War 2. In the Korean War, its text was updated for the jet era by the substitution of tailpipes, turbines, burners and the like for the earlier engine components. The endurance of this song may owe something to the way it mocks disaster by making it a subject for laughter as well as to whatever rapport pilots might have with the machines on which their lives depend.

> A handsome young airman lay dying,
> At the end of a bright summer day;
> His comrades had gathered around him
> To carry his pieces away.
>
> The aircraft was stacked on his wishbone,
> His machine gun was wrapped round his head;
> A spark plug he wore on each elbow,
> It was plain that he'd quickly be dead.

He spat out a valve and some gaskets,
And stirred in the sump where he lay;
To mechanics who round him came sighing,
These are the brave words he did say.

"Take the magneto out of my stomach,
And the butterfly valve off my neck;
Tear from my liver the crankshaft—
There's a lot of good parts in this wreck.

Take the manifold out of my left eye
And the cylinders out of my brain;
Take the piston rods out of my kidneys
And assemble the engine again."

The notion that the pilot's relationship with his aircraft calls for nothing less than a total union is an example of technique in the sense used by Robert S. McCarl. He describes it as "the shaping principle of an organization" because the way it is transmitted from one group to another forms the basis for the prevailing concepts as to what constitutes a particular type of work (1978:149). Within the particular occupation this is called "knowing the trade," being a "good mechanic" or "a good hand." In this case, the criterion of "good pilot" is defined by "The Dying Aviator" and many other songs as requiring a complete rapport with the aircraft. It becomes part of "the pattern of manipulations, actions and rhythms that are the result of the interaction between an individual and his or her work environment and that are prescribed by the group and used as criteria for the determination of membership and status within it" (McCarl 1978:149).

Boyne and Thompson (1986:130) even describe a highly experienced pilot as "flying in his mind," so that "the airplane did what he wanted it to do, his body merely being an interfacing mechanism." Some of the songs of fighter pilots in the Vietnam War treat this intimate relationship between operator and machine with an almost mystical lyricism. This treatment is epitomized in a song by Dick Jonas about a fighter-bomber known as the Thud (an abbreviation for the F-105 Thunderchief). The singer sees his plane as an extension of his body, with himself as its brain. (See Getz 1981; and Tuso 1971 and 1990.)

The intimate relationship between a crewchief and his helicopter is described rhapsodically in an occupational narrative that was still circulating in manuscript form among Vietnam veterans in 1988. The machine was used to retrieve wounded in "dustoff" operations and was personified as "Mercury, the messenger from the gods" because to the wounded it appeared to be from Heaven. To the crewchief it was his home in which he slept at night.

Cleaning her filters, changing oil and parts that started showing wear, washing the blood and mud off, I kept her healthy. I fed her every few hours, for her turbine drank a gallon a minute. . . . Quicksilver was more than a helicopter—an experience I am proud of and will never forget. How close can a man get to a machine?[7]

The occupational base for much military life clearly demands the happy warrior's skilled devotion to the actual tools and instruments of war. Thus, the *Gunners' Handbook*, a manual distributed to all members of the Royal Regiment of New Zealand Artillery, reminds them that the guns are "an emblem to be kept bright and free from all reproach" and that they are always to be treated with respect and dignity. An artillery cadence in the U.S. Army says, "Tell my baby to forget about me because I've got a new lover, the Artillery" (Johnson 1983:76).

Similarly, the recruit infantry soldier in most armies is ceaselessly instructed that his rifle is his best friend and that it must be treated with zealous care. He is encouraged to think of it as a component of himself. Consequently, the rifleman's creed, cited in a novel about the U.S. Marine Corps (Hasford 1979:23), states that the recruit's rifle is human because it is his life. He will have to learn it "as a brother" and keep it clean and ready so that they will become part of each other.

A slang term for penis is "weapon," so it is not surprising that another maxim of the U.S. training depots recognizes the soldier's penis as cognate with his rifle.

> This is my rifle, this [penis] is my gun;
> This is for fighting, this [penis] is for fun.

But if weaponry has a masculine sexual identity, why are aircraft, ships and vehicles always personified as "she"? Kenagy (1978), in a discussion of the sexual symbolism of aircraft, perceives a duality in which, when the aircraft is in the air, it seems to become a physical extension of the pilot's body and his masculine virility, while, at the same time, in Freudian terms (and like a ship or a vehicle) it is hollow, uteruslike, able to be penetrated and able also to disgorge its contents. Whether or not this complex ambiguity is accepted as an explanation for the connection between the warrior and his machines, there can be no doubt that the relationship is close and often very emotional.

A song circulating in the U.S. Navy in the 1930s declares that "a good old greasy submarine is home sweet home to me."[8] The Maori Battalion which fought in World War 2 in the N.Z. Division's campaigns in the Middle East and Italy from 1941 to 1945 became so attached to a bullet-riddled truck that was used as a mobile canteen that at the end of hostilities they shipped it 12,000 miles back to the homeland where it reposes in a museum. It is just possible to envisage somebody developing a comfortable nostalgia for a canteen and even for "a good old greasy submarine," but it is difficult to imagine how anyone could cultivate a tender relationship with an armored vehicle. Nevertheless, J. Glenn Gray (1959:81) cites the example of a German soldier at Stalingrad bursting into tears on learning of the destruction of his tank, an event that meant more to him than the loss of comrades. The practice of assigning nicknames (especially feminine sobriquets like "Memphis Belle," "Circe," "Big Bertha," "Anzio Annie," "Moaning Minnie," "Matilda Lou" and "Milwaukee Babe") to guns, jeeps, aircraft and ships confirms that there is more than a strictly utilitarian connection between the warrior and his weapons and transport.

The occupational life of people in the services has parallels with that of other kinds of workers who are locked into disciplined routines and the performance of standardized duties in conformity with the techniques of the assembly line. These instinctively try to humanize their situation. Abrahams (1978:25–26) points to the importance of repeated pranks and joking among people doing highly routine and repetitive work in ways that "both articulate and undermine the status system if only for the moment." He also cites a case study that describes how people maintained their sanity with the aid of joking and stalling techniques "on the line" and how they developed "a sufficient sense of common cause" by off-duty drinking sessions that heightened their special sense of group identity.

This is similar to what happens in the military environment as a reinforcement of its established receptivity to ideological conditioning, traditional services lore, ceremony, rituals, specialized jargon and the experience of belonging to a high-risk and isolated occupation that has many resemblances to the work groups of seamen, cowboys, lumberjacks, whalers, miners, railroad workers and prison occupants. The singing of songs, the resort to improvised self-entertainment, the exchange of jokes and humorous narratives, the performance of pranks and the recital of cautionary tales are typical features of the expressive behavior that characterizes life in the ranks.

Like the folklore of farmers, loggers and cowboys, these forms of cultural expression also have a seasonal periodicity bound up with the work cycle. However, the wartime military work cycle revolves around the mounting of offensives rather than being solely determined by the seasonal rhythms of climate. In this respect, people in the services resemble the tugboat men studied by Byington (1985:37) whose lives were determined by "always erratic and unpredictable ship schedules." In their case work and play were necessarily divided, but in the life-journey of the soldier, sailor or airman, the division is less demanding and more a matter of spontaneous opportunity.

Services life can also be enlivened by experimentation with deviancy.

As many of the songs in this survey will indicate, the male-dominant environment of the wartime services (especially in the ranks) has almost unlimited opportunities for resort to bawdiness, grumbling, violent satire, heavy drinking, drug-taking, black market trading, sexual license, theft and other forms of minor crime. This places low-status military "workers" in much the same position as gang members, pirates, political revolutionaries, protesters and other organized groups who find it convenient to operate outside or close to the boundaries of law. On the other hand, not everyone is given to such extreme methods of deviancy and may be more attracted to the possibilities that their particular duties offer for acquiring a personal reputation for professional competence, reliability and commitment to the mission or the work in hand inside the task groups and artificial communities of the armed services. It is a curious irony that archaic and tradition-bound organizations, licensed to employ almost unlimited violence against the wartime enemies of the state, and tolerant of much personal aggressive fantasy and sadism, should be a refuge for the survival of some of the integrative ideals of community and responsibility that are so attractive to the moral conscience.

The military's occupational culture also contains alternative responses to the power of the machine. Some songs, as well as some doggerel recitations and jokes, are protests against fate and the workings of the military authority system. Others are a form of licensed joking about the prospects of death or wounding and the distrust of authority. Still others are fantasies in a licentious comedy of manners that has been able to flourish unimpeded in what is largely a male-dominant cultural enclave. They are couched in a comic irony that permits the jocular and frequently obscene utterance of otherwise unpalatable or intolerable truths. Such a response to military life is a kind of dark laughter in which the long and deadly saga of endurance of the ordinary combat soldier is memorialized. Echoes of that laughter enrich many of the songs that have been compiled in this book.

As far as an individual participant is concerned, the difference between war and peace may be merely one of degree. The wartime situation imposes extra restrictions on personal behavior and for some participants introduces spectacular hazards into the performance of tasks. Frontline soldiers come under psychological stress, partly from the repetitive anxieties of combat and partly from the tedious spells of boredom and inactivity that typify much military life. Such ordeals are not unique to wartime; they are inherent to a less spectacular but equally oppressive extent in the daily routines of any modern industrial society. Warfare concentrates, accelerates and dramatizes them. Modern war, in other words, is industrial production speeded up and intensified. Men and women are exploited and consumed in this process just as they are in other mass production industries. War as a method of consuming expendable units of human life is no more illogical, surprising or deadly than, for instance, the consequences that the liquor, tobacco, automobile, illicit drug and fast food industries have for some of their addicted clients.

Any harmful aspects these products might have are likely to be obscured by the rhetoric of advertising. The military environment achieves a similar reduction of the sinister by naming tanks, guns and aircraft with affectionate symbolism. The idea is to reduce their lethal qualities by the device of personification which confers a degree of humanization on their terrible impartiality. Yet the mechanistic and alienating nature of modern warfare is explicitly recognized in both popular literature and folklore.

For example, a German gunnery officer, the hero of a novel about World War 2, ruminates over his dedication to the industry of destruction and perceives himself as "a cog in the wheels of the murder machine, a worker in a factory producing human corpses" (Kirst 1974:68). The process of systematic, mechanized death reaches one of its pinnacles of accomplishment in the artillery barrage that is timed very precisely to the movements of infantry engaged in set-piece attacks of the kind brought to catastrophic perfection in World War 1. By this means, many hundreds of thousands of more-or-less voluntary human units were destroyed in that war, as were some impressive numbers in World War 2. To this must be added the casualties from large-scale bombing raids, including the nuclear destruction of two Japanese cities. War as a means of consuming its participants (who now include entire civil populations) represents the ultimate triumph of the machine over humankind and supplies a provocative demonstration of the demonic potentialities unleashed by the industrial revolution.

These potentialities can be illustrated from the resources of folklore. In the fantasy of "The Steam Arm,"[9] a nineteenth-century ballad about the adventures of a soldier who lost an arm at Waterloo, the amputee has an artificial limb manufactured like an iron beam which is operated by "a compound of clockwork and steam." He uses his device to deal with his wife who has been beating him, with the result that "before she had time to wink she lay flat on the floor."

Then he returned and rapped at his door,
He rapped in steam raps half a score,
The arm in power grew more and more
Until bricks, board and mortar all strewed the floor.

At length he left his home outright
And now he wanders like a sprite;

He neither gets rest by day or night
For the arm keeps moving with a two-horse might!

Then there is the comic variant of the fable of the sorcerer's apprentice
which was current among British and Commonwealth troops in both
world wars and still circulates in America. This is "The Great Big
Wheel."[10] It is a bawdy ballad, sung to the tune of "The Old Hundredth,"
a melody that has been traced back to the sixteenth century.[11] It describes
the frustrations of a soldier who devises a mechanical apparatus consisting of "two brass balls and a bloody great wheel" with which he plans
to satisfy the omnivorous sexual appetite of his wife. This monster is
equipped with "a tool of steel"; and the whole outfit is driven by steam.
Of course, it proves uncontrollable, and its client-victim comes to lurid
destruction under its ministrations. G. Legman (1968:369) notes the
element of helpless inevitability in all such sex-machine fantasies and
comments in a further discussion (1978:748) on "the sensation of being
impotent, a castrated creature in the face of the Machine."

This sadomasochistic parable of a death machine devouring its individual victims is paralleled collectively on the battlefield by the larger
spectacle of a whole civilization caught up in the murderous complexities
of military technology. According to Martin Van Creveld (1989:1), "war
is completely permeated by technology and governed by it." Hence, the
wheel as a symbol of civilization and the technology it has created are
also the source of its torment and possible doom. Its perverted use
illustrates the paradox of twentieth-century technology which destroys
as it liberates. Soldiers are its raw material, even though, as Gray points
out (1959:179), some of them are able to take an integrative pleasure in
coordinating their movements and daily activities in "the proper func-
tioning of the instruments of war."

But war is not yet fought exclusively by robots. It continues to present
its human participants with problems of adaptation and survival that are
similar to what they might encounter in sawmill, factory, shop floor, coal
mine, meat processing works or any other mass production industry—
except that in the military context their survival difficulties may be intensified because of the denial of many of the normal comforts and
assurances of domestic life as well as their inability to take a day off or
a holiday whenever inclined. Along with these constraints goes the frequent necessity to lead a deprived, frontierlike existence in barracks,
field or frontline. In that case, a winter tour of duty on the Russian front
in World War 2, tenancy of a slit trench in the Libyan Desert in 1941,
an infantry patrol in the frozen landscapes of Korea, or a complex and
dangerous mission in the jungles of Vietnam becomes an educational,
thought-provoking experience with implications that may be more spec-
tacularly urgent than the occasional crisis of factory or workshop. Be-

cause the oppressive workings of the machinery of death are so evident and threatening, the combat soldier becomes more emotionally dependent on the supportive qualities of his squad or subunit (which takes the place of the industrial production team), on the leadership of those he trusts, and on the reassurances and exhortations of whatever versions of the popular culture he is exposed to.

As the first comprehensive survey of its kind, this book treats military occupational song as any kind of singing or chanting that is known to have circulated among military groups and has originated either within the services or has been adapted from the resources of popular culture, especially the vast number of musical parodies of popular songs and adaptations of their lyrics that proliferate in the military as a vigorous part of the folklore–popular culture matrix.

The example of "Bless 'Em All" has already been mentioned. Another can be seen in the recorded versions of "Lili Marlene" that were widely played and sung by commercial entertainers throughout occupied Europe during World War 2. However, the parodies of the song that the troops on both sides of the battle lines composed and circulated contained sentiments that were often very different from the platitudinous original. In order to examine the expressive attitudes displayed in this and many other similar compositions, a thematic approach has been developed for this book. It ranges from cohesive enthusiasm for official goals and eager compliance with the military system by the happy warrior, to the comic philosophy of grudging endurance and joking about military life expressed by the reluctant warrior, along with the indulgent fantasies of the bawdy warrior. The grumbling of the hungry warrior is dealt with in a chapter about food, while the problem of death is explored in a treatment of the concerns of the mortal warrior. Finally, some of the songs and entertainments of the Vietnam warrior are treated in a concluding chapter.

NOTES

1. For example, the expression of anti-Americanism by disgruntled allies in World War 2. See Cleveland (1984).

2. "Songs of World War II," *Variety*, Vol. 10, November 1965.

3. Ibid.

4. American Red Cross (1945:25).

5. See Jack Santino (1992) for an account of the development of the custom of displaying flags, yellow ribbons and other "war-related assemblages."

6. See Dolph* (1929); Getz (1981); Palmer* (1944); Sandburg* (1927); Smith* (n.d.); Wallrich (1957); and Ward-Jackson (1945).

7. "The Story of Quicksilver," collected by Professor Lydia Fish at the Vietnam Veterans' Memorial, Washington, D.C., in 1988. The full text is located in

the archives of the Vietnam Veterans Oral History and Folklore Project at Buffalo State College, New York State, and also in the Cleveland Collection.

8. "Submarine Song," Western Kentucky. See Appendix.

9. Gordon Collection, c. 1924, LC.

10. Babad* (1972); Cray (1969 and 1992*); Getz (1986a); Hart (1971); Hopkins* (1979); and Silverman* (1982).

11. Cray (1969:198 and 1992:393) in a discussion of the theme of "the great big fucking wheel or machine" traces the tune to sometime before 1554 in Geneva.

2

The Happy Warrior

The wartime services are a favorable site for transmitting occupational culture. Not only are they dedicated to regimental and other traditions and customs, but also their environment fosters the passage of military lore from one generation to another. It is also highly receptive to entertainers and performers. Most wartime units are likely to include someone who can play a musical instrument and who can remember the popular song hits of the day as well as a range of traditional items learned from civilian life. Some of these performers may compose or adapt the occasional piece to express their personal moods and feelings, but for the most part they rely on the content of the popular culture and are likely to parody simple, well-known tunes that can be easily remembered and do not require much musical skill to reproduce. So "Sweet Betsy from Pike," "The Tarpaulin Jacket," "John Brown's Body," "Yankee Doodle" and "The Yellow Rose of Texas" have been ready-made conveyances for generations of soldiery attuned to the lyrical possibilities of the musical stock of the popular culture.

For instance, many British soldiers' songs of World War 1 used hymn tunes because they were well known, had few melodic or rhythmic complexities and could be easily sung on the march. For similar reasons, country-western tunes like "The Martins and the Coys" and "Home on the Range" were used by New Zealand troops in World War 2. In Vietnam, U.S. troops relied on commercial hits like "Riders in the Sky," "Truck Driving Man," "Tiger by the Tail," "Downtown," "I Walk the Line" and "I've Been Everywhere," as well as old familiar tunes like "The

Wabash Cannonball," "Casey Jones" and "The Wreck of the Old 97" to compose their parodies. Each generation draws on the popular idiom of the day in its music-making.

The chief sites for singers and composers working in the services have usually been the military camp, the troopship or the unit billet or bivouac. In the Vietnam War, officers' and NCOs' clubs were an important location where unit singers and instrumentalists could perform. There were no limitations on the spread of materials from one formation to another. Copies of songs could either be handwritten, typed in the orderly room or circulated by mimeograph and photocopier. Hundreds of air force unit songbooks have been produced by such means. In Vietnam, where the portable tape recorder went to war with the troops, a song or a whole concert could be recorded, copied and easily distributed. The widespread use of helicopters made it possible for entertainers and singing groups to travel rapidly from one area to another.

Military songs also have an intergenerational and international fluidity. An outstanding example of this characteristic is "The Dugout in Matruh" (Cleveland 1959*, 1961 and 1975*; Page 1973). This song is a comic account of life in the British Eighth Army during the desert campaigns of World War 2, sung to the tune of "The Little Old Log Cabin in the Dell." Matruh is an abbreviation of Mersa Matruh, a seaside village near the border of Egypt with Libya. It was used as a supply base for desert operations in the North African theater. The area was a rendezvous for the N.Z. Division in the confusion that followed the Eighth Army retreat from Tobruk in 1942. The survivors of this retreat equated Mersa Matruh and its arid surroundings with heat, monotony, thirst, flies, confusion, military incompetence and bombing raids, but in this song the happy warrior is ironically inspired to make the best of things.

> Oh I'm just a greasy private
> In the infantry I am,
> And I've a little dugout in Matruh
> Where the fleas play tag around me
> As I nestle down to sleep,
> In my flea-bound, bug-bound dugout in Matruh.
>
> *Chorus*:
> Where the windows are of netting
> And the doors of four-by-two,[1]
> And the sandbags let the howling dust storm through;
> I can hear that blinkin' Eytie[2]
> As he circles round at night,
> In my flea-bound, bug-bound dugout in Matruh.
>
> Oh the floor is littered round
> With bully and meatloaf[3]

For marmalade and jam we never see,[4]
We're a happy little band
In this bloody land of sand
In my flea-bound, bug-bound dugout in Matruh.

Where the windows etc.

Oh I wish I had a sheila
To sit upon my knee
To share with me the misery that I'm in,[5]
For I'd woo her and caress her
If this her home she'd keep,[6]
In my flea-bound, bug-bound dugout in Matruh.

Where the windows etc.

Now there's Messerschmidts and Stukas
Flying all around,
Hurricanes and Spitfires very few,[7]
When the bombs and shells start flyin'
That's where you'll find me lyin'
In my flea-bound, bug-bound dugout in Matruh.

Where the windows etc.

"The Dugout in Matruh" has some obvious connections with a song in Colquhoun* (1972) which circulated among shearers and the rural workforce of Australia and New Zealand. In this song the "poor old shearer" is as happy as a clam in a land of ewes and lambs in his "tick-bound, bug-bound dugout in the True," and so on.

The True is a rhyming synonym for the Blue, an Australian slang term for any remote and underpopulated district where huge spaces of empty and often vividly clear sky confront the lonely resident or traveler. The exact nature of the connection between the two songs is unclear, but the flea-bound, bug-bound dugout at Matruh may have been inspired by the shearer's tick-bound, bug-bound equivalent. Both have resemblances to an American composition, "The Little Old Sod Shanty," and would appear to be parodies of it.

White (1975:167–75) describes some of the family of songs that developed from "The Little Old Sod Shanty" and attributes its tune either to W. S. Hayes's "The Little Old Log Cabin in the Lane," composed in 1871, or possibly to J. C. Chamberlain's "The Old Log Cabin in the Lane," published in 1875. The claim on which each sod shanty was situated was a 160-acre grant of free government land set aside in the Midwest for settlement. Since timber was scarce, the walls of the shanty were made of sods cut from the prairie, with door and window frames fashioned from packing cases. Life in such earthy quarters was not unlike the primitive experience of living in a wartime dugout or slit trench.

White cites several sources for the words of "The Little Old Sod Shanty" and reproduces a text taken from the reverse side of a period photograph of a typical sod dwelling.

> I am looking rather seedy now while holding down my claim,
> And my victuals are not always served the best,
> And the mice play slyly round me as I lay me down to sleep
> In my little old sod shanty on the claim.
>
> Yet I rather like the novelty of living in this way,
> Though my bill of fare is always rather tame,
> And I'm happy as a clam, on this land of Uncle Sam,
> In my little old sod shanty on the claim.
>
> The hinges are of leather and the windows have no glass,
> While the roof, it lets the howling blizzard in,
> And I hear the hungry coyote as he sneaks up through the grass
> Round my little old sod shanty on the claim.

The song continues with an account of the disorder in the shanty and a wish that "some kind-hearted Miss" would take pity on its occupant who would bless her "if thus her home she'd make."

The parallels between the sod shanty and the dugout are evident. The mice playing slyly have become fleas playing tag. Windows without glass become windows of netting, hinges of leather are doors of four-by-two, the hungry coyote sneaking through the grass has become the Italian Air Force circling round at night and some kind-hearted Miss is converted into an antipodean "sheila."

As an expression of comic dismay at the hardships of frontier or frontline conditions, parodies of this song have traversed several occupational fields in at least four regions of the world during a period of about 100 years. Its most recent appearance in 161 Battery of the Royal New Zealand Regiment of Artillery in Vietnam, however, is less a testament to resignation than a declaration of the happy warrior's superior powers of endurance. The battery was part of a composite New Zealand and Australian force that operated in Phouc Tuy province. The following is from the Cleveland Collection.

> Oh I'm just a greasy gunner
> From One-Six-One, I am,
> And I've a little dugout in Vietnam,
> But the boys, they took no notice
> As they nestled down to rest
> In that flea-bound, bug-bound dugout in Vietnam.
>
> I wish I had a Maori girl
> To sit upon my knee,

To give me all the comforts I have lost,
But the boys etc.

The Captains and the Colonels
Are stuffing us around;
Sarge, he says the bombs are everywhere,
But the boys etc.

They're firing H and I[8]
At Charlie all night long,
Victor Company's got them on the run,
But the boys etc.

Soldiers' songs often proliferate under the influence of particularly memorable tunes that become vehicles for a range of compositions on widely differing subjects. A notable example is the transnational deployment of the melody of "Lili Marlene," one of the outstandingly popular songs of World War 2. It was listened to, played and sung in various languages by the German, British and U.S. contestants throughout Europe, and it generated an extensive family of parodies, adaptations and improvisations.

For instance, a commentary on the predicament of the Wehrmacht on the Eastern Front entitled "In dem western Moskaus" ("To the West of Moscow") likened the fate of Adolf Hitler to that of Napoleon before him (Henderson c.1945). At least one bawdy version of "Lili Marlene" in which the singer imagined himself having sexual intercourse with Lili circulated among German Afrika Korps troops in the Middle East. Eighth Army soldiers fighting in Italy borrowed the tune to compose a bitter satire about being called "D-Day Dodgers." New Zealand troops in Italy used it to present a list of grievances to their prime minister and to demand that since they had seen and done enough, they should be taken home. A U.S. Fifth Army version of this appeal for repatriation addressed itself at the end of the Italian campaign to President Truman.

Please Mr. Truman, let the boys go home,
We have conquered Naples and liberated Rome;
We have subdued the Master Race,
There are no Krauts for us to face;
Oh please let us go home,
Let the boys at home see Rome.

We've met the Seventh Army at the Brenner Pass,
We've had hepatitis, and shrapnel up our ass;
We don't want to fight the Japs,
Give the job to the low-point chaps;
Oh please let us go home,
Let the boys at home see Rome.

We've drunk our way through rest camps, Sorrento to Rome;
We're tired of signorinas, we want no more to roam;
Just send us back to the U.S.A.,
We'll give up all our overseas pay;
Oh please let us go home,
Let the boys at home see Rome.[9]

The reference to not wanting to fight the Japanese dates the composition of this particular text to the period after the cessation of the war against Germany on 9 May 1945 and before the end of the war against Japan on 14 August 1945. "Low-point chaps" were soldiers who had low priority for repatriation because their time overseas had been insufficient for them to have reached a qualifying level on a points system calculated according to duration of service. Another version (from the Underwood Collection) relating to the postwar occupation of Germany by U.S. forces was directed at "old Mr. Truman" and complained that

We slaven in Frankfurt,
We slaven in the home;
Drinking Schnapps and drinking wine,
Auf wiedersehn Fraulein....

During the postwar occupation of Germany, soldiers of the U.S. First Division used the same tune to compose a cynical account of the fraternization process and its acceleration with the aid of soap, chocolate, chewing gum, cigarettes and supplies diverted from UNRRA (the United Nations Relief and Rehabilitation Agency), which was responsible for feeding a considerable part of the population of occupied Europe.

Nights in old Ansbach
On the promenade,
You can see the Maedchen
And see them being made;
Come mit mir Fraulein
I've got it bad,
I'll give you soap and Schokolade,
And fix it with MG,[10]
And fix it with MG.

Cigarettes for Papa,
Kaugummi for me,
Ich war never Nazi
And Heil to Liberty;
I need more ration points for Ma,
Then I'll say to you, "Ja, Ja."
That's what you want, nicht war?
That's what you want, nicht war?

In Hotel Bleiborn
I know a cute D.P.;[11]
She weighs 250
And gives it all to me;
She is Polski through and through
And never says "I no can do";
UNRRA it's up to you,
UNNRA it's up to you.

Hans was in the Wehrmacht,
Got his discharge pass;
They stamped PW[12]
Across his Aryan ass;
Now he is burning when he sees
His Fraulein on the G.I.'s knees;
She sure looked nice with hair,
She'll look like hell all bare!

In a 1949 parody, Lili Marlene herself becomes part of the spoils of Allied victory. The G.I. (with the aid of plenty of cigarettes and chocolate) is able to obtain five minutes with her for 20 marks.

Unter in dem keller
Mit ein schön soldat,
Beaucoup zigarette
Und viel schokolade;

Zwaunzig mark
Für funf minute,
Das ist prima,
Das ist gut
Mit dir Lili Marlene,
Mit dir Lili Marlene.[13]

The people who composed and performed such songs were ordinary soldiers whose ability to recite, play a musical instrument or sing provided them with an additional role to fulfill within their various units. The present writer himself acquired some of the World War 2 material cited in this book in the course of a random history of informal performance and music-making while serving in the N.Z. Division in World War 2. There is pleasure in such performing as well as the satisfaction of playing a key part in the group's expressive life.

Singing usually occurred at rowdy, improvised gatherings when the platoon was out of the frontline and billeted in a rest area. In Italy this always involved drinking large quantities of wine looted from vineyards or from peasant farmhouses. When the writer joined his battalion, his first performance was with the aid of a guitar that had been purchased in Cairo and laboriously carried all the way up to the front. The company was billeted in a block of apartments a few miles behind the lines. It was snowing, but a fire had been lit in the stove of what remained of somebody's kitchen, and a drinking session was under way.

The wine had been looted from a vermouth factory. It was stored in five-gallon Jerrycans that had previously contained petrol. These were placed in a snowdrift beside the front door. Before consumption the liquor was preheated, a Jerrycan at a time, on the stove. Under the influence of hot, tinned Vermouth laced with petrol fumes, the gathering launched into a rendering of "O'Reilly's Bar" (Brand* 1960; Cray 1969* and 1992*; Silverman* 1982). This was followed by "The Good Ship Venus" (Babad* 1972; Cray 1969* and 1992*; de Witt 1970; Silverman 1982) and by "Fuck 'Em All."[14]

People were attracted from the other platoons billeted nearby to join in the choruses, to swap rumors, to talk about the fortunes of mutual acquaintances and to exchange personal experiences. The company commander paid a visit and bravely drank some of the appalling mixture in the Jerrycan. Later, the singers extended themselves to "Salome" (Getz 1986a; Silverman* 1982) and "Hey Jig-a-Jig."

"Hey Jig-a-Jig" was to become the platoon's big song, performed in unison at most celebratory occasions with the addition of verses extemporized by anyone who cared to contribute. It parodied a wartime popular hit entitled "Hi-Jig-a-Jig, Hi-Jig-a-Jig, Follow the Band." The theme of this song was the comic, off-duty relationships with their domestic consorts of a succession of people in various occupations, beginning with a sergeant who is "the tyrant of Company B" except that when he comes home in the evenings "he has to take orders from me." The chorus was a repetition of the phrase, "Hi-jig-a-jig, follow the band." The platoon soon reworked this song into a parody of military life. A USAF version that features colonels, majors and captains is reproduced by Getz (1986a). Cray (1992*) has several versions derived from "My Husband's a Mason," which he traces to the early eighteenth century.

As a signature tune, "Hey Jig-a-Jig" had no merit other than its juvenile simplicity and its comic reversal of the conventional standards of military propriety in a drunken game that signified that, in spite of their incorporation into the military machine, the revellers still had a fragmentary expressive life of their own. Historically, they had been propelled into a struggle against facism and nazism, while socially and culturally they had bound themselves together in group attestations of solidarity, celebrated in the fellowship of drink and song and put periodically to practical test on the battlefield.

The essential requirement of all such songs was that the temporary community should be able to join easily in their performance. Solo items were usually listened to, but they lacked this element of spontaneous participation. There were cowboy songs like "Red River Valley" and "Home on the Range." There were a few Australian ballads like "Waltzing Matilda" and "Maggie May" as well as "Blue Smoke" (a nostalgic reminder of rural New Zealand) and several Maori songs. Sometimes the platoon sang "Isa Lei" (a Fijian expression of the sorrows of parting) along with a few romantic, popular lyrics picked up in wartime Italy like "Mama," "Amor, Amor, Amor," "Besame Mucho," "Bianca Stella" and "Rive la Banda" (a rallying song against the *Fascisti* which was popular with the Italian resistance).

The fraternity of talk in the platoon was greatly encouraged by the fact that the battalions were recruited and subsequently reinforced on a regional geographic basis. As a result, sometimes the entire male youth of a rural settlement might be decimated, but it made friendships easier to establish and it provided an inexhaustible substratum of gossip, scandal, kinship, reminiscence and folklore for leisurely exchange and exploration. Men who came from the same township or hamlet could always discuss a common network of mutual friends, relatives, acquaintances and work relationships. Liquor and song were the catalytic ingredients for the relaxed atmosphere in which this kind of homely discourse flourished, along with much rumor, speculation and prediction about the battalion's future, the course of the war and our own immediate situation in it. Much of this discourse centered around accounts of people's adventures on leave and their exploits with women. Italian towns were rife with prostitution, and many solders eagerly sought sexual encounters. The other compelling topic was what happened in the last attack.

The platoon had undergone a demoralizing experience. It had been almost wiped out when it was caught near the start line by a barrage from its own supporting artillery. Some of those who were hit had been carrying phosphorus smoke grenades clipped on their webbing or stowed in its pouches. Shrapnel hits on their bodies exploded some of the phosphorus, scattering its fiery liquid over others who came to their aid. Some died of wounds, and others were hospitalized with lengthy treatments for burns. Each survivor had a different perspective on this grisly affair, which was reopened like a never-ending postmortem every time one of the victims returned.

Jack Santino (1978:202–4), in a study of occupational narrative, describes a type of accident story that is persistent over time and consistent over occupations. Its object is to teach the reasons for accidents and how they can be avoided in the future. As a cautionary tale, the phosphorus burns episode had two imperatives: don't carry these explosives in an attack, and don't get caught in the open in a barrage. Other stories recounted by survivors emphasized the importance of never going into an attack without equipping yourself with one of the short-handled, broad-bladed shovels favored by infantry in case it became necessary to dig a trench in a hurry. One should also never get into a truck with a loaded magazine on an automatic weapon because several soldiers in the platoon had been wounded when the butt of a Tommy gun slammed against a steel deck with sufficient force to start it firing, even though the safety catch was on and there was no bullet in the chamber.

From time to time, other casualties from earlier periods in the life of the platoon turned up from hospitals or from convalescent depots. These men had stories that went back to the savage battles at Cassino and Orsogna in the early days of the Division's involvement in the Italian campaign. From these men, recent arrivals learned about the group's past and about who had been notable in it. These personal narratives gave a sense of historical continuity and accountability to the men's immersion in ordeals that otherwise seemed like the random workings of chaos.

Not every group of 2NZEF soldiers was quite so exposed to morbid spectres from the past. Sometimes a singsong had a simple, nostalgic enjoyment. The diary of a transport driver records one typical occasion on 16 May 1942 in Syria.

Feeling fed up, tired of war and homesick, but will see it through. In the evening, Alan Reeves got out his fiddle and played some decent music which was most helpful. We finished by having a musical evening aided by a mouth organ and a band of tin mugs, steel helmets etc.[15]

Experienced performers could exert an influence that went far beyond the boundaries of their own units because they would sometimes be invited to attend festive events held by other outfits. In their audiences there might also be visitors from other formations and nationalities. Men of very diverse origins were to be found in military camps and on troopships, and this was especially the case with the British Eighth Army in which songs like "The Dugout in Matruh" and various parodies of "Lili Marlene" quickly achieved wide currency.

The Pacific theater in World War 2 offered similar opportunities to entertainers. A typical composer of services songs was Peter Ferguson, a soldier in the 30th Battalion, 8th Brigade Group, 2NZEF, which garrisoned Fiji early in the war. He explained that

We had no wet canteen as such in the early days but a sort of compound where we bought bottles of warm Aussie beer. . . . I don't actually recall many singsongs in the canteen, but I remember that most of them were held in our Public Works Department type of two-man huts. Perhaps we were allowed to take our bottles out of the compound, or else we smuggled them out so the vocal cords could be oiled back in the lines. I composed the ditties myself and sang them at these singsongs in the huts, and I dished out some hand-written copies on request. From these sources the songs gradually spread through the battalion.

They were written to well-known tunes rather than as verses to be fitted later to tunes. Country-western songs that were popular before the war like "The Martins and the Coys," "Rocking Alone in an Old Rocking Chair," and "I'll be Hanged If They're Gonna Hang Me," were already well-known so I expect it was natural to fit words to them. We had no organized camp concerts or entertainments so we made our own. In B Company it was usually myself, Togo Ashwell on the saxophone and Mac McEwan on the spoons. The Denly boys were in H.Q., I think. Later we got Brown of Taramoa as guitarist, and later still Jack Warren on piano accordion. My own guitar got smashed in a hurricane, so after that things depended on Togo's sax. . . . I think the surroundings and the company plus the circumstances led to the birth of these songs. This, of course, is why so much has come out of shearing gangs and similar back-country associations of men for whom there are few distractions from boredom.

In addition, most groups have at least one chap who has a pleasing voice, and though most of us are inclined to associate isolated groups of men with ribald ditties, in point of fact on many occasions, if a good singer is present, the preference is likely to be for songs with nostalgic sentiment. I've often heard a good song being sung in the camp lines of an evening while gradually the noise drops and everyone listens. But being men to whom sentimentality is a sign of weakness, perhaps we also welcome the association of bawdiness with masculinity—the tough image.[16]

When the troops who had been on Fiji were sent as reinforcements to the Middle East and Italy, they carried with them some of these Pacific songs and gave them a much wider currency. As well as providing a means for sending lyrics across considerable distances, the services are also a vehicle for conveying traditional lore across time from one generation to another. Veteran instructors in training depots impart some of the service lore they have acquired to successive intakes of recruits. Military formations go to great lengths to perpetuate their various customs, traditions and rituals through drilling, ceremonial parades and the singing of officially endorsed songs. Many of these reinforce the solidarity of in-groups because they employ an esoteric terminology of allusion, slang and technicality which is understandable only to those with appropriate "on-the-job" experience.

An example of this esoteric exclusiveness can be seen in a Vietnam War song entitled "The Black Iron Cross." This is one of the items sung by the Merrymen in Lansdale* (1976). The Merrymen were a group of officers in the 173rd Assault Helicopter Company which was stationed at Lai Khe with the 3rd Brigade of the Ist Infantry Division. They performed at concerts and social functions. The song contains language that is peculiar to the brigade, beginning with the distinctive black cross emblem. This came about when the 3rd Brigade commander had a black cross painted on the helipad so that it was more visible from the air. It resembled the German Iron Cross of World War 1 and World War 2, and for this reason the 3rd Brigade became known as the "Iron Brigade." Its personnel adopted the black cross as an informal insignia that they wore on their fatigues. The Ist Division is known as "the Big Red One," a sobriquet it acquired in France in World War 1. The song describes how the men who wore the black iron cross as the crest of the Iron Brigade fought the Vietcong "on danger's path."[17] Led by the "Hocking Six,"[18] they lived up to their motto of "For Duty First"[19] as they fought for freedom "for the rest."[20]

Services songs also impart technique. Specifically, they present judgments about what constitutes a particular kind of work and what might be considered the qualities of a "good" soldier, sailor, aviator or whatever. Such a person is more than somebody who is skilled in the technicalities of the occupation. He must also be accepted by the group as a person whose behavior conforms to its expectations and experience of the work situation and of the attributes of whomever it is prepared to admit into such a category of competence. As a statement of technique, "The Black Iron Cross" expects the "good" 3rd Brigade member to display the offensive spirit and to put duty first in spite of hunger, heat and thirst.

Similarly, the "good" pilot in a helicopter assault company was expected to carry whatever cargo he was assigned to any destination and to actively engage the enemy in the process. "Army Aviation," sung to the tune of "Oleana" (Broudy 1969), under the slogan "All the way, night and day," expounds a philosophy of coming back for more and more in a stressful and hazardous occupation.[21]

There is a close similarity between the performance standards of firefighters as described by McCarl (1985:28–29) and the status allocation process in an infantry platoon. In both cases, to apply McCarl's dictum, "each individual establishes a reputation in the culture by anticipating the critical appraisal of fellow workers and developing a niche for himself." Thus, among experienced and aggressive combat infantry in World War 2, the critical appraisal of fellow "workers" meant readiness to attack, steadfastness under fire, doing a fair share of whatever tasks had to be performed, looking after one's weapons, using them skillfully and showing an intelligent concern for the fate of others in the interests of common survival. The laconic comment "he's a good soldier" summarized all these virtues and was the highest praise that could be awarded in this particular occupational circle.

The occupational lore of groups is important in the life of the soldier. It is structurally incorporated in all military organizations by virtue of their reliance on small basic units like the infantry section or squad, the aircraft, naval or tank crew, or the gun team. These are the sites for the occupational culture of any army or any other services organization. They are also the environment in which the work skills of drilling and marching as well as training with weapons, equipment, aircraft, naval vessels or any kind of transport or machinery are taught. Services songs are sensitive to perceptions of how these skills are to be applied.

This can be seen in the cadence calls of the U.S. military. Cadences are officially approved, organizationally compatible songs and chants that help define the techniques of the military work group. They are performed either to a strict marching tempo or to a rapid, double-time measure, according to the speed at which the formation is required to move. Their most obvious purpose is to coordinate the motion of a body of troops by keeping them in step and helping them to reduce fatigue and prolong endurance. In doing so, however, they also teach the importance of dedication to the mission whether it be withstanding a powerful and frightening enemy, attaining some strategic objective, finishing a long route march or completing some other irksome assignment to the expected standard of performance. The system of training and instruction imparts the actual skills of the military trade, but cadences supply some of the psychological conditioning needed to put them into successful practice.

An Armoured Corps call (Johnson 1983:85) declares that its guns are made for shooting and when they get a mission they'll "drill a hole" in the target. An infantry cadence, which has the soldier running 10 miles in the early morning, describes the army infantry as a running machine (Parallex* 1986a). This song echoes the mechanistic view of the soldier as a robot in a process that demands discipline as the prerequisite for all other aspects of technique.

Cadences also inculcate respect for tradition. A Marine Corps parody of "That Old Time Religion" (Parallex* 1986b) praises the Marine Corps spirit, which is said to have been good enough for Chesty Puller and Dan Daly (distinguished former members of the Corps). Such testimonials also emphasize the qualities of a "good" marine as a proud, fearless, dedicated warrior who is mythologically descended from Daniel Boone, Davy Crockett and other frontier heroes.

> Born in the backwoods, raised by bears;
> Double-boned jaw, three coats of hair;
> Cast-iron balls and a blue-steel rod;
> I'm a mean mother-fucker, I'm a Marine, by God![22]

Some cadence calls also feature heroic models whose fantasies of power and aggression have more in common with the exploits of war film and comic book stereotypes than with military actualities. Several of the cadences cited by Johnson (1983) describe Airborne Rangers as wanting to live a life of danger, suggest that enemies could be dealt with by a combination of shooting, beating, kicking, face-stomping, strangulation and bludgeoning and threaten to bomb Iran and to use nuclear weapons if American hostages were not released.

Such aggressive simplifications are part of a calculated acculturation to violence resembling the "premium on masculinity" with its accompanying boxing, wrestling, gymnastics, tackle football, social pressure to drink and the vigorous pursuit of the opposite sex described by Thorpe (1967) as obligatory for the indoctrination of the fledgling military pilot. It is similar in purpose to the bayonet-fighting drills and competitive body sports programs inflicted on recruits in the British and Commonwealth armies of World War 1 and World War 2. These were intended to produce stereotyped responses to threats or crises and to desensitize the soldier to the moral questions behind the use of language advocating face-stomping, bayoneting and other techniques of close physical combat.

Desensitization is also a strategy for dealing with anxiety. Cadences are helpful for this purpose. They are an officially approved body of doctrine that deals in convenient certainties that help reduce the range of anxieties confronting a recruit. Yet, as psychological conditioning for the field, too fanciful a hyperbole of aggression may be counterproductive when the actualities of combat are experienced and the happy warrior discovers how frail and vulnerable he is. Perhaps this is why a few of the Vietnam War cadences contain more realistic insights about such matters as being the target for incoming fire when all you want to do is hit the ground (Johnson 1983:143).

The happy warrior has two faces. One of them shows some awareness of his vulnerability and the lowly life he leads, and the other reflects the romantic stereotypes of popular literature and the recruiting poster. Both are exemplified in two nineteenth-century ballads. "The Regular Army Man" is a realistic view of the U.S. soldier as no gold-laced hero parading with cockade and posing with a gun, but rather as someone who wears a crust of tan and leads a very rough life in which

> There ain't no tears shed over him
> When he goes to war,
> He gits no speech nor prayerful "preach"
> From Mayor or Governor;
> He packs his little knapsack up
> And trots off in the van,
> To start the fight and start it right,
> The reg'lar army man;
> The rattlin', battlin',
> Colt or Gatlin'
> Reg'lar army man.[23]

The alternative perception of the happy warrior as a kind of dashing frontier hero emerges in a fragment of a U.S. Cavalry song entitled "Hurrah for a Good Suit of Blue." This song tells us that

A ship's band improvised by the crew of a British battleship in World War 1. (*The Auckland Weekly News, New Zealand, 12 August 1915. Courtesy of The New Zealand Herald.*)

The band of the 69th Regiment, 165th Infantry Division, AEF, on its return from World War 1. (*National Archives*)

An instrumental group at Fort Belvoir, Virginia, January 1943. *(Library of Congress)*

Corporal C. Bedford of Surrey, England, playing a captured German accordion in a British Advanced Dressing Station on the Garigliano River, 20 January 1944, during the Italian campaign. *(National Archives)*

German Afrika Korps soldiers in a transit camp in Naples in 1943. (*National Archives*)

Grunts, a satirical war comic, depicts many of its characters in animal form. In this episode the Dogfaces are being harassed by a Vietcong sniper. *(Reproduced from "Mekong Delta Blues," story and art by Jim Groat, in* Grunts, *issue No. 1, November 1987, published by Mirage Studios. Courtesy of Jim Groat.)*

An entertainment for patients of the U.S. 69th General Hospital while in transit on the Brahmaputra River in Southeast India, 8 June 1944. *(National Archives)*

Pfc. Frank Williams, combat engineer, 173rd Airborne Brigade, playing his harmonica during a lull in operations in the highlands of Dak To, Vietnam, November 1967. *(U.S. Army)*

The life of a soldier is wild and romantic
While serving out on the West frontier....
Then hurrah for a good suit of blue,
A pistol, a horse, and carbine too,
We're off to the mountains, the woodlands
And the prairie
To pass a wild and reckless life away![24]

Something of this exuberance has survived into modern times in the songs of U.S. aviators. These extol the flyer's aggressive spirit and his dedication to an ideal of heroic achievement. In "Faith of the Army Air Force" (Getz 1981), the tie that binds men in the air is said to be "a rock-like faith...a religion of the Air Force of the fighting U.S.A." Thorpe (1967) has described military flying as an act of faith in the sense that it calls for absolute trust in the machine as well as in the whole environment of aviation. He also draws attention to the status enhancement of flyers who, on surviving serious accidents, became the center of attention and adulation at Friday night drinking sessions at the base where they were being trained.

Under combat conditions in the Vietnam War, the extended opportunities for heroic dramatization were revealed in dozens of narrative ballads that describe pilots as Fighter Jocks, Gunslingers, Sons of Satan, Wolf Packs, Red River Rats, Mach Riders, Vagabonds of Vietnam and the like. Dick Jonas, a Vietnam War fighter pilot and a prolific composer of songs about air combat and the epic qualities of pilots, in "The Battle Hymn of the Red River Rats" (Getz 1981; Jonas* 1987b) describes an idealized code of honor. The warrior is to hold his head high, stand tall, never run from a fight and sing the Red River Rats' Battle Hymn.

This epic flamboyance and heroic presentation of self are not universal among military aviators and may illustrate a tendency to theatricality and hyperbole that is characteristic of the American popular culture. By comparison, the songs of British airmen seldom indulge in such self-dramatizations and concentrate mainly on the treatment of life in the services as a ribald comedy of manners expressed in a tradition of laconic understatement. Talk of faith, death or glory by Fighter Jocks and Mach Riders would be dismissed in the British air services and their Commonwealth counterparts as mere line-shooting heroics.

Whatever the individual perceptions of the warrior might be, as an important part of the life of any society, the military share its popular culture and adapt elements of it to suit their special occupational requirements. For example, the cadence tradition in the U.S. armed forces is an outcropping of popular forms of entertainment. Johnson (1983) attributes the origins of "Sound Off" chants to a black soldier named Willie Duckworth at Fort Slocum, New York, in 1944. Their basic structure consists of a line sung by the drill leader, followed by variations in which the troops either repeat it, reply with a verse of their own or count cadence. It can be done in quick time or in double time as the troops move in formation together. The combination of verbal improvisation and rhythmic versatility in these chants may owe much to the musical accomplishments of American blacks as well as to the American stage tradition of song and dance.

The stage musical is a powerful, indigenous, American popular art form that has at its core a blending of music and dance, with a chorus line that performs carefully choreographed maneuvers with elaborate precision. There is a similarity between these dance routines and the evolutions of the parade ground. Both require strict obedience to tempo and the performance of disciplined movements in unison. Although production of a musical comedy stage show requires a great deal of beauty and talent, it also needs an almost martial precision, demonstrated in the drill-like movements of the chorus line as it performs its rapid, repetitive, squadlike dance routines as spiritedly as any formation of barrack-square virtuosos. There is no essential difference between the Rockettes and an army drill team giving a demonstration on Armed Forces Day. Matters of choreography and costuming apart, both offer precisely drilled performances that are entertaining to large numbers of people.

In addition to its prospects for eurythmic diversion, military life also offers opportunities for dressing up and giving dramatic performances. The ceremonial aspects of service discipline and tradition with their passion for parades, drills and the display of uniforms, decorations, badges of rank and unit insignia are an importation of dramatic stylistics from the worlds of theater and fashion designed to invest the wearers with presentations of self that are consistent with concepts of martial behavior and regimental pride and distinction. The warrior, like any experienced actor, has a repertoire of dramatic roles to perform. Each role requires careful costuming and sufficient rehearsal to make sure that public performances convey the correct impressions. The dress uniforms that are worn for such occasions are a way of inflating pride in the masculinity and status of the wearer as well as conforming to the requirements of the dramatic context.

Alison Lurie (1981:18) draws attention to the anonymity of uniforms and their signification of membership of some group. They are a variety of clothing that follows what she calls the principle of camouflage. The drab khaki, blue, grey or olive hues adopted by many armies are certainly consistent with the earthy trenches and battlefield landscapes in which twentieth-century wars have been fought while their stiff, regular outlines correspond to the organizational and behavioral rigidities of military discipline.

Lurie also comments that the uniform is a sign that we need not treat someone as a human being, but this observation overlooks the chief advantage of uniformity. The convenience of mass supply apart, this is simply the expectation that the wearer will be treated, and will treat people, in a standardized and predictable way. Such orderliness and drab utility, however, make contrast and decoration the more striking. The wearing of colored or polished insignia, service ribbons, medals and badges become the more distinctive and theatrical. Indeed, as women penetrate the military services in increasing numbers, will style, flair and sophistication transform the utilitarian purpose and appearance of uniforms? Will legs, breasts, hair, teeth, boots, buckles, belts and cosmetics become more prominent features of military dress? Will drilling, marching and uniforms present even greater opportunities for bodily display and choreographic elegance?

Full dress parades and military displays are also an opportunity to demonstrate the military establishment's proficiency at drilling, its skills with weapons and equipment and its readiness as guardians of national security. The changing of the guard ceremony at Buckingham Palace is a world-famous exercise in public theater that dramatizes the principle of readiness and precision as it invokes the color and spectacle of the British military past. In the case of the U.S. armed forces, the showmanship of similar public occasions is a powerful feature of American popular culture that has long been animated by a tradition of festivity and carnival through such agencies as the circus, the musical comedy stage, community parades and civic celebrations.

Since the advent of satellite technology, television has become a global stage for mounting public displays of military strength directed as much to arousing popular support as to ensuring the discomfiture and defeat of enemies. Whatever its strategic compulsions might have been, the Gulf War was a carefully managed popular culture production designed to demonstrate the overwhelming superiority of U.S. offensive capacity and the skills of its soldiery in destroying their opponents' military infrastructure while themselves sustaining minimal losses. Viewers of newscasts were highly exposed to the formidable features and physique of the U.S. force commander, General Norman Schwarzkopf, who soon became popularly known as "Stormin' Norman" and "the Bear." On his victorious return to the homeland from "Operation Desert Storm" he became a top attraction for parade and celebration organizers, beginning with the biggest ticker tape parade in New York history and followed by the official victory parade in Washington, D.C.

Warfare and the military are also popularized through film, popular literature and comics. Their staple ingredient is epic fantasy centered on characters with whom audiences can readily identify. Williams (1990:104) notes that comics "feed the dream images of the readers" and "reflect the values, fears and expectations of society." As adventure narratives, war comics describe violently aggressive incidents in which heroic warrior stereotypes do battle against the forces of evil to help their comrades, save the nation from defeat and protect it from perils. The heroes of these fables rely on the stock ingredients of the folktale— a mixture of audacity, cunning and strength augmented by magic and the occasional intervention of the supernatural. They take the place of the Indian fighter of the frontier, the gunslinger of the Wild West or the Teutonic warrior of ancient times.

Some stories contain examples of the haunting of battlefields by dead leaders and the performance of miraculous and marvelous feats by warriors under supernatural protection. The heroes of these tales undergo fear tests and illustrate the virtues of patriotism and manliness as they exemplify the characteristics of the male American warrior. He has to overcome his fears, he doesn't stand for bullies or dirty tricks and he is versatile. Like any frontiersman he can turn his hand to anything, and he is resolute enough to put aside the concerns of his loved ones when stern duty calls. Anybody can be a hero, and in a crunch, any enlisted warrior can take over a situation, demonstrating the democratic ideal that officers are not essential and anyone can be a leader.

The adventures of these paragons suggest that resolute collective action by teams of dedicated men and women can solve problems, defeat enemies and triumph over evil by the use of a mixture of technology and legitimate violence. This formula proved inadequate for dealing with the Vietnam War. Early 1960s and 1970s Vietnam War comics featured heroic U.S. soldiery engaged in a crusade against communism, but by the late 1980s they were responding to changed popular perceptions of the nature of the conflict. A Marvel Comics publication entitled *Nam* adopted a more ambiguous, inconclusive and at times unheroic treatment. Fantasy was subdued in favor of documentary realism both in artwork and in narrative content.

Its hero is an ordinary young soldier in a typical infantry outfit. His adventures are presented objectively, with little patriotic idealism or exaggerated heroics, and there is no romanticization of war. The story concentrates on the occupational techniques of being a soldier and avoids the problem of taking sides in the debate over the war's justification and its strategic management. This approach is connected with the emergence of a body of neutral public opinion that has slowly taken shape through film, literature, radio and the folk music of Vietnam veterans, and has also grown around such dramatic mediatory icons as the Vietnam Veterans' Memorial in Washington D.C.

The American frontier, with its gunfighter and cowboy heroes, has been a prolific source of warrior stereotypes in American popular culture. In his discussion of the mythmaking output of the producers of national popular culture, Slotkin (1985) analyzes the dominant themes of a frontier myth that conceives of American history as a heroic-scale Indian war, with its central concern being the problem of what happens when the end of the frontier is reached. At the core of the myth is a belief that progress can be maintained only by "the heroic foray of civilized society into the virgin wilderness, and by the conquest and subjugation of wild nature and savage mankind" (Slotkin 1985:531). Slotkin recognizes the applicability of this paradigm to Western history as a whole, and in the metaphoric excesses of wartime ideologies, it is not difficult to visualize the labeling of the enemies of the nation-state as representatives of "savagery" engaged in decisive struggles over the future of civilization on battlefields that offer unlimited possibilities for violent frontier-style heroics.

Psychologically, war provides a field for frontier behavior by soldiers freed from the constraints of modern urbanized life. The frontier (in its transposition to frontline) offers a rangeland for personal experimentation in violence by those who have been nurtured in the doctrines of competitive individual achievement. On the military frontier, they are licensed to operate as so many "bounty hunters," "Indian fighters" or "gunslingers" according to their individual talents and opportunities.

The fact that war is good for big business adds further impetus to the rush to the frontier. The commercial interests that have prospered in a series of twentieth-century wars have benefited as much from the slaughter of millions as earlier investors profited from the opening up of new global territories and industries based on the exploitation of colonial and New World natural resources and labor. War is a major feature of all Western economies, offering a "fatal environment" for enactments of a mythology in which the agents of technocratic, democratic civilization struggle against savagery and endure the prospect that victory requires the extermination of at least one, and possibly all, of the contestants.

In World War 2, G.I. Joe, the Dogface Soldier and Grunt were the symbolic inheritors of the American frontier warrior tradition, but no new heroic stereotypes emerged in Vietnam because the moral inversions of the conflict made alien invaders out of U.S. soldiers in a cause that was not generally perceived as sacred and in which they could not portray themselves as champions of civilization.

Popular perceptions of the warrior are also shaped by the self-images that gain wide currency through wartime journalism. As occupational metaphors, these range from the romantic fantasies of aviators to the more earthy, ironically derogatory insights of the infantry soldier. In World War 1, American troops were known as "Doughboys." The origin of this term is obscure. Winterich (1931) attributes it to the flour ration issued to troops in the American Civil War. Partridge (1970) ascribes it to the large, globular, brass buttons of the Civil War infantry uniform.

Other writers think it may have originated in the dough-like mud that Sherman's foot troops had to negotiate during their famous march to the sea.

British soldiers in World War 1 were called "Tommies," a diminutive of the fictional character of Tommy Atkins. In newspapers, weekly magazines and booklets circulating on the home front, the British Tommy was depicted in the character of "Old Bill." This caricature was drawn by Bruce Bairnsfather, a wartime illustrator. It exhibited phlegmatic qualities of indifference to danger and a capacity for ironic endurance of the hazards and deprivations experienced by the British working class in its four-year ordeal of violent death and suffering in the trenches.

Nothing approaching this intensity of emotional experience was evident in World War 2 when the ordinary British soldier was described as a "Squaddy" (a member of a rifle squad, the basic unit of the infantry) or as a "Pongo" (a term of obscure origins, perhaps deriving from the Indian Army). His German equivalent was *der Landser*, but there appears to have been no tradition of soldierly caricature in the Wehrmacht. The works of Jaroslav Hasek, a Czechoslovakian writer who wrote an antiwar satire entitled *The Good Soldier Schweik*, were banned in Nazi Germany where a massive propaganda effort was directed toward bolstering the identity of the soldier as an obedient and dedicated instrument of the regime. A Soviet writer, Alexander Tvardovsky, published a sequence of narrative poems about Vasili Tyorkin, an ordinary Russian soldier who engages in the epic struggle against fascism. His adventures are in no way critical of the command or of the regime, though unofficial versions did circulate, for instance, about the court martial of a soldier who farted at his post.

In World War 2, George Baker's "Sad Sack" (derived from the contemptuous designation, "he's a sad sack of shit") appeared as a regular feature in the U.S. Army newspaper *Yank* and survived as a comic strip into postwar life. It was made into a film in 1957 with Jerry Lewis, David Wayne and Peter Lorre, and a CBS/Fox videofilm version of it appeared in 1984. Sack was the helpless, apathetic, incompetent, slow-witted victim of the U.S. military machine and its aggressive tyrants. He was a perpetual loser as well as a candidate for every indignity. He epitomized the conversion of the soldier into a kind of suffering beast of burden whose only protection was dumb endurance as he humped impossible loads of stores, did menial fatigues, dug holes, blundered in and out of danger and floundered from one absurd, unfair situation to another at the whim of fate and bureaucracy.

The British edition of *Yank* also featured the adventures of Artie Greengroin, an enlisted man with a long, thin nose and a tapering chin that had a permanent cigarette drooping from it. But the most potent image of the U.S. soldier in World War 2 was that of the G.I. This term began as an abbreviation for "Government Issue" but became the national stereotype for American soldiery anywhere in the world. Dave Breger's comic strip, "G.I. Joe," was featured in both *Yank* and *Stars and Stripes* (another U.S. Army paper). G.I. Joe had a youthful, zestful innocence that carried him from one comic situation to another. Authority was usually shown to be ridiculous, but seldom vicious or overbearing as it nearly always seemed toward both Sad Sack and Schweik, the distant, literary progenitor of all representations of the oppressed, suffering conscript. G.I. Joe retained his symbolic power as a warrior image into the postwar world.[25] In 1983, $80 million worth of G.I. Joe toys were sold in the United States. These were plastic, miniature models of U.S. soldiers and equipment in combat locations, while a Marvel comic book series celebrated the adventures of G.I. Joe as "a real American hero."

Some of the most penetrating studies of the psychology of the happy warrior were contained in the cartoons of Bill Mauldin in *Stars and Stripes* (a U.S. Army newspaper). Some of Mauldin's work annoyed the brass, but in his view "a soldier's newspaper should recognize only two restrictions—military security and commonsense. Outside of that it should devote itself solely to being a paper that will provide soldiers with good news coverage and a safety valve to blow off their feelings about things" (Mauldin 1944:32). His characters were Joe and Willie, infantrymen who had "been in the war a couple of years" and looked like it. They were always dirty, unshaven, tired, apprehensive and cynical, particularly about the activities of the rear command, authority of all kinds and people who weren't in the infantry.

Their chief characteristic was a laconic facility of understatement. This is the essential weapon of satiric comment employed in all oppositional jokes, folksongs and cartoons directed at military organization. As a chronicle of laughter about danger and misery, the adventures of Joe and Willie demonstrate the enduring power of the comic spirit, while as stereotypes of national identity they illustrate the ambiguity of popular culture content. Joe and Willie are scornful of incompetence and all forms of military "bull," but they are dedicated frontline soldiers who keep on fighting whatever their cynical insights might be. They exhibit the same unassuming integrity as "Grunt" and "Dogface"—two other occupational images that perfectly reflect the lowly status and expectations of the ordinary combat soldier. As role models, all of them possess something of the frontier fighter's bravery and skills as they set themselves apart from those with softer, less dangerous jobs in the rear. As status distinctions, such images are also a source of pride that helps the warrior resist absorption into the uniform anonymity of mechanized war. They are a protest against the commodification of the soldier, just as the wartime creation of fantasy creatures like "Gremlins," "Squimps," "Spandules" and the mysterious "Kee Bird" (who haunted the wartime military bases of the Arctic Circle crying "Kee, Kee, Keerist but it's cold") helped humanize the mechanistic routines of World War 2 by peopling it with beings who were magical as well as comical.

Discussion of the qualities of the happy warrior should not overlook the reality that in wartime not everyone leads a life of spectacular aggression or even notable activity. For instance, a Seabee stationed at Eniwetok Atoll in 1944 observed that he never thought he would have to spend his time listening to complaints from officers that their refrigerators weren't working, their beer was getting warm and they couldn't get ice for their cocktails. "Also I never expected my function would be to relay complaints from officers that their toilets didn't flush because somebody had thrown empty liquor bottles down the drain. War is hell, isn't it?"[26]

Some songs reflect a desire for status recognition by groups who perform humdrum tasks that don't allow them to dramatize themselves in the same terms as the combat warrior. This is evident in "The ground Crew Song" which draws attention to the skills of the maintenance staff who keep aircraft operational. It was collected from an engineer officer in the 504th bomb group, 20th U.S. Air Force, on Tinian which he described mockingly as "the garden paradise of the Pacific" in World War 2.

> They dream of the pilot so daring
> As he gracefully soars through the air,
> But without all the boys of the hangars
> He wouldn't be flying up there.
>
> Oh give me a wrench and a pliers,
> The will and the spirit is there;
> If a thing has two wings and an engine,
> We'll fix it to fly in the air.
>
> So hurrah for the men that maintain them,
> The oilers and grease monkeys too;
> Our motto and name—"Keep 'em Flying"
> Three cheers for the Army Ground Crew.[27]

Similarly, a song about the U.S. Merchant Marine from World War 2 draws attention to its unrecognized but essential service. The U.S. Defense Department did not award Americans who served in the war the official status of veterans until 1988.

> From the bulge of an old Hog Islander
> To the decks of a new C-3,
> You often find us wondering
> Why the hell we went to sea.

Why the hell we left our girls behind,
Why we left that home-cooked chow,
If we had to do it over again
We'd be in the Army now.

Oh if the Army and the Navy
Ever see a battle scene,
They would know their guns were brought to them
By the U.S. Merchant Marine.[28]

In the male-dominant culture of the armed forces, women are particularly affected by status differentiation. Therefore, it is not surprising to find the songs of female members of the Marine Corps in World War 2 defining the culturally sanctioned ways in which their somewhat constricted tasks could be completed. "March of the Women Marines"[29] accepted a subordinate role for women who were to serve so that "men may fight in the air, on land and sea," while as "Lady Leathernecks" (the title of another song) they were dedicated to winning peace so as to "bring our men home again."[30]

Some of these songs vented the women's "disillusionment with military life" (Burke 1992), but most were in compliant alignment with what was expected of the World War 2 female warrior. Women's Army Corps (WAC) songs collected in World War 2 from U.S. training camps speak of training hard to take the place of men "who'll be free to fight the Axis" and of the necessity to stand behind the army where "Athena's banner will soar," making history with the "swish, swish, swish . . . of the petticoat army." Another song entitled "Company Six" (to the tune of "The Battle Hymn of the Republic") asserted the determination to succeed by excelling at the training routines in force at Oglethorpe, a World War 2 training school for WACs in Chattanooga, Tennessee. To the spirited tune of "The Man on the Flying Trapeze" its occupants promised to be good soldiers even if it took years.

In comparison, women serving in a British Auxiliary Territorial Services (ATS) antiaircraft battery in England during the blitz in World War 2 were able to express a more militant perception of the role of the female warrior because they were directly committed to the hazards of the battle for control of the air. A song to the tune of "The Ferryboat Serenade" (Page 1973) describes the operation of the Sperry predictor which computed the position of a target and brought the guns to bear on it. The ATS operator loves to work a Sperry and details her movements and reactions "while bringing down a Jerry."

Today's female warriors in their march toward gender equality would be likely to take a much more adventurous view of themselves. During the last two decades, increasing numbers of women have been integrated into the armed services of most Western nations where they have moved from lowly occupations as cooks and clerks into a broad range of jobs that in wartime would take them much further into danger. This process has been particularly expansive in the U.S. forces where there has been an accompanying debate about the extent to which women should be allowed to engage in combat.

Attitudes toward the presence of women at the front are determined by a combination of necessity and the prevailing images of the popular culture. These traditionally assign primacy to the male warrior whose participation in combat is seen as the supreme test of manliness. This excludes women because as idealized occupants of the homeland they are to be defended and cherished. Admitting women to the frontlines undermines the cultural assumption of male superiority, removes the monopoly of heroism from male control and disposes of the simplistic division of wartime society into an aggressive, masculine military force on the one hand, and a home front of passive, noncombatants supporting the frontline warrior on the other.

The popular songs of World War 1 and 2, and the folklore of the troops themselves, illustrate the strength of these attitudes. However, about 10,000 women served in Vietnam, mostly as nurses but also in various specialist capacities. They received very little recognition. A great many more U.S. and British servicewomen took the field in the Gulf War. Eleven died in combat, two became POWs and several were wounded. The experience resulted in the lifting of a ban on U.S. Air Force and Navy women flying planes in combat. At the time of writing, however, this was as close to the frontline as women were, in theory, allowed to go. They were still not acceptable as combat infantry, and there is not much indication that popular cultural perceptions have shifted on this question.

Throughout history, individual women have distinguished themselves in combat. For example, Mary Ludwig Hays shared the rigors of Valley Forge with her husband John Hays and saw action at the battle of Monmouth in 1778. She carried pitchers of water to swab the bores of overheated cannons and quench the thirsts of the gunners who dubbed her "Molly Pitcher." She also rescued a wounded soldier and later took her husband's place in the gun line and kept his cannon in action when he was wounded. In recognition of her heroism, General Washington issued her with a warrant as an NCO, and she became known as "Sergeant Molly." This legend is celebrated in the traditions of the 7th Field Artillery Association which issues an "Artillery Order of Molly Pitcher," to be worn as a medallion with formal dress uniform.

A women's "Death Battalion" saw service with the Czarist Russian forces in World War 1. Women also fought in the Soviet and Yugoslav partisan armies of World War 2. For cultural reasons, however, the male warrior is still preeminent in his citadel of aggressive manhood. Whether women in combat would find it necessary to sing the sort of songs and engage in the kinds of aggressive, ritual behavior that characterize male participation in military life seems doubtful. However, the evidence from one of the few studies of gender integration in a unit deployed under extreme conditions of physical stress (Devilbiss 1985) does tentatively suggest that male-female bonding of a nonsexual nature occurs readily enough in a dangerous environment.

However they define technique and allocate status, the songs of the masculine happy warrior help to integrate him in an envelope of shared identity that is rich in the details of his particular group's language and experience. The more demanding and violent fields of action open to male soldiery have always encouraged them to parade their identities in the language of zestful physical aggression. For instance, in 1941 this boast (to the tune of "A Son of a Gambolier") was circulating in Camp Claibourne, Louisiana. By changing the name of the service cited in the first line, the song can be made to suit almost any group of singers.

> The Infantry, the Infantry
> With dirt behind their ears;
> We lick our weight in wildcats
> And drink our weight in beers;
> The Artillery the Cavalry,
> And the God-damned Engineers
> Could never beat the Infantry
> In a hundred million years![31]

A similar composition, "The Cannoneers," is an adaptation of a satire against "The Pioneers" (Cray 1969* and 1992*; Mackay 1927). An air cavalry cadence (Johnson 1983) declares that the singers' trademark is guts and pride with an ambition to be "above the best." All the many versions of such songs circulating among the military are dim echoes of the ancient epic tradition of the warrior proclaiming his boastful prowess before doing battle and declaring his warriorlike superiority in the overcoming of "tests."

Whatever the situation of the military work group, its songs will advertise its feelings of identity and solidarity in terms that are appropriate to its concepts of technique, whether this celebrates the deeds of gunslingers, wearers of the Black Iron Cross, aspirants to "guts and pride," members of a petticoat army or foot soldiers with dirt behind their ears. The self-identification of the happy warrior can also be intensified by condescension toward outgroups. Cadences cited in Johnson (1983) claim that infantry wish they were artillery, the army is proud of its history and USAF aviators are the best "above all the rest." However, the integratory functions of military song override such distinctions, although the content of the songs and the way they are performed may vary considerably.

For instance, U.S. Army cadences are prolific in slogans like "Airborne—all the way!" "One—two—three—four! I love the Marine Corps!" "Armor is a wall of steel" and "Cavalry is the army's shield." Recruits are expected to learn the cadences circulating in their various corps and to make the required responses when called upon by drill instructors. The U.S. cadence tradition is one of the chief ways in which knowledge of the past and of the ideals of service in a particular unit are taught to recruits. Cadences are usually sung on the march and are a unique form of expressive behavior that originated in the U.S. Army. However, most armies have a tradition of singing on the march, mainly because their commands equate it with a relatively contented state of mind on the part of their troops and regard it as a useful morale-building activity.

In some armies, singing on the march has been carefully programmed into the training and performance of the happy warrior. This reached a peak in the German Army of World War 2 whose soldiers were expected to know a range of officially approved items. Most units had a standard routine for determining what was to be sung and exactly when. There was much to choose from; for example, *Deutsches Soldatenleiderbuch* (Stoffregen 1943), a pocket edition of items for field use in the Wehrmacht, contains 114. The publisher's foreword states that the German soldier and his songs were inseparable parts of a unique integration. A penciled list compiled by the former owner of a copy of this publication (now in the possession of the present writer) indicates that he had learned at least twenty-six of them as a member of the Hitler *Jugend* before he actually entered the Wehrmacht.

In contrast to this industry of military socialization, British and Commonwealth armies show little inclination to encourage their troops to sing officially authorized songs. This is because their understanding of technique leans more in the direction of tight-lipped understatement rather than heroic self-inflation and regimental hyperbole. In addition, their political cultures tend to regard military service as an occasional unpleasant necessity rather than a dedicated act of devotion to the state. Singing among British and Commonwealth troops has therefore been mainly voluntary and inclined to reflect the sentimental popular lyrics of the day when it is not engaged in comic protest, satire, grumbling and the composition of anarchic, oppositional parodies.

NOTES

1. According to B. F. ("Mick") Shepherd, a World War 2 veteran of Auckland, New Zealand, an alternative version is "where the walls are made of hessian and the windows four-by-two" (Correspondence: Shepherd to Cleveland, 29

December 1975). Shepherd points out that the standard size for timber framing during wartime was 4 inches by 2 inches by whatever length was appropriate. As for the dugout, it could be a comic reference not to a slit trench or some kind of sandbagged position, but to a troop's latrine. "A dugout has no windows, nor does a latrine, but *if* it had them they would have a four-by-two frame. The walls would be of hessian and the doors would let everything through." Shepherd dates the earliest known performance of this song in 2NZEF as 6 September 1940, the day the force's First Echelon landed in Egypt.

2. A reference to the Italian Air Force.

3. Bully beef and meatloaf were two varieties of tinned rations supplied to the troops *ad nauseam.*

4. The reference to marmalade and jam in the version cited here is a confusion of fact. Rations in 1940 consisted of a staple of bully beef, meatloaf and baked beans. Jam was almost nonexistent, but Palestinian marmalade was plentiful—too much so "as we hated the sight of it" (Shepherd to Cleveland, 29 December 1975). For this reason, Shepherd believes that the text reproduced here from the Cleveland Collection is from a period later than 1940.

5. Sheila is a New Zealand or Australian colloquialism for a female. This is a reference to the sexual frustrations of the soldiery. Cf. Page (1973:70): "To ease me of this awful pain I'm in" and Shepherd: "To free me of the pain that I am in" (Shepherd to Cleveland, 29 December 1975).

6. Cf. Page (1973:70): "And much as I do love her, how I wish that she were here" and Shepherd: "Oh that girl, how I would love her if she'd only live with me" (Shepherd to Cleveland, 29 December 1975).

7. The mention of Hurricanes, Spitfires, Messerschmidts and Stukas is further evidence that this is a post–1940 text. These planes were not in use then on the North African front. There were difficulties for a long time in even getting Spitfires off the ground because in the desert heat the fuel vaporized before it reached the carburetor and suitable modification was very slow. Stukas and Messerschmidts did not appear until the German Afrika Korps became active in the desert in 1941.

8. Harassment and interdiction fire directed at routes and locations likely to be frequented by the enemy.

9. Underwood Collection.

10. Avert prosecution by the military government for fraternization, which was banned for several months when the occupation began. The text is from the Hamilton Collection.

11. A displaced person cared for by UNRRA.

12. Hans, a German soldier who is still technically a prisoner of war, reacts to fraternization by shaving the heads of German girls involved.

13. Indiana.

14. Otherwise known in its bowdlerizations as "Bless 'Em All." Variants appear in Cleveland 1985*; Cray 1969* and 1992*; de Witt 1970; Getz 1981 and 1986a; Hart* 1971; Hopkins* 1979; McGregor 1972; Silverman* 1982; Tate 1982; Wesley Ward 1966.

15. Cleveland Collection.

16. Ferguson to Cleveland, 30 April 1973.

17. The Ist Division's telephone code was "Danger"; thus, its 3rd Brigade fought "on Danger's path."

18. According to former members of the formation, the 3rd Brigade commander used the expression "hocking" as a euphemism for the descriptive adjective "fucking." "Six" in U.S. military terminology is any unit commander from company level up.

19. The motto of the 3rd Brigade is "Duty First." The divisional motto is "No Mission Too Difficult: No Sacrifice Too Great: Duty First." "Duty" was also the telephone code for the 3rd Brigade.

20. Presumably the rest of the free world.

21. In addition to its observations about technique, this song invokes the guiding spirit of deceased predecessors. In a tape-recorded performance (Broudy* 1967), the singer begins with a solemn, spoken declamation that dedicates the song to "all those aviators who have gone before us in this conflict here in Vietnam." In its concluding verse, it modulates into an elegaic gesture to the dead. The cultural meaning of this song is that the warrior does not live by technique alone; he seems also to need some reassuring spiritual or supernatural endorsement that places him in a continuing tradition of idealized service.

22. "Marine Marching Song" taught to recruits in a boot camp in Texas, 1982 (Berkeley).

23. Gordon Collection, LC.

24. Gordon Collection, LC.

25. It is a masculine image that may now be unsuitable as a military stereotype, though some writers have been referring to the female warrior as "G.I. Jo." In World War 2 the problem became apparent as increasing numbers of women were recruited. Agnes Underwood, in her 1947 research into G.I. language, recorded in her field notes that "G.I. Jill" and "G.I. Jean" were in use along with "Winnie the WAVE." U.S. WAVES (an acronym for Women Accepted for Voluntary Emergency Service in the Navy) developed their own wartime slang. Coveralls were "blitzpants," girdles were "hipkits," coats were "tents." When a slip was showing, "a booby trap was sprung" and bras issued to females in the Marine Corps were "G.I. coconuts."

26. Letter dated 17 December 1944, D. V. Smith correspondence, Underwood Collection.

27. Hamilton Collection. Getz (1986a) has a variant.

28. Indiana. Collected in 1949. The tune is unknown. A Hog Islander was a vintage freighter built at Hog Island, Delaware. A C-3 was a cargo vessel, the second of four original types designed by the U.S. Maritime Administration at the beginning of the 1930s. They were fast (16 knots), with a gross cargo capacity of 8,000 tons. Because of their speed some were converted into flat tops and troop transports. (See La Dege 1965.)

29. Indiana.

30. Indiana.

31. Indiana. Variants appear in Dolph* 1929; Cray* 1992; and Palmer 1944.

3

The Reluctant Warrior

Not every wartime soldier is burning with patriotic zeal or inspired with resolute determination to engage the enemy. In the armies of Western democracies, the reluctant warrior can accept the inconvenience and personal disadvantage involved in compulsory service for the state as long as he is able to grumble, protest and joke about his fate, to ridicule his leaders and to assert his personal autonomy and dignity. As the poetry of the relatively powerless, soldiers' songs are one of the few means at their disposal for the uninhibited expression of their anxieties. Those who live under close military discipline are in much the same predicament as the occupants of any absolutist regime. They cannot openly challenge its power, nor can they freely express their dissent and anger. Only in ribald song, surreptitious jokes and satiric fantasy can the truth about their feelings be given a brief exposure.

Comedy, especially in its ironic forms, institutionalizes the doubts and fears of the reluctant warrior by allowing him a degree of furtive, ambiguous expression. As a variety of what H. D. Duncan (1962) has called "sanctioned disrespect" it permits soldiers to endure and even to mock what they cannot change. At the same time, it also asserts what Langer (1953) calls "the vital rhythm of self-preservation" by allowing the fear of death or injury to be more openly acknowledged without shame or embarrassment in the guise of laughter.

The classical statement of the comic philosophy of self-preservation has been current in the British Army, probably since the Napoleonic Wars in the song, "I Don't Want to be a Soldier." U.S. troops in World

War 2 called it "The Picadilly Song," and variants circulated among the Marine Corps in the South Pacific in 1943.[1] It was also known to some of the U.S. troops in Vietnam, judging by a rendering that is included in Lansdale* (1976).[2] All versions derive their humor from a contrast between the perils of battle and the sexual pleasures of life back in England. The reluctant warrior declares that he would sooner lead the life of a pimp than be shot or injured by a bayonet thrust. The following is the World War 2, Marine Corps version.

Monday I touched her on the ankle,
Tuesday I touched her on the knee,
Wednesday with success I lifted up her dress,
On Thursday her chemise,
Gorblimey!
Friday I put me 'and upon it,
Saturday she gave me balls a tweak!
But on Sunday after supper,
I ran the 'ole thing up 'er
And now I'm payin' seven and six a week,
Gorblimey!

I don't want to be a soldier,
I don't want to go to war,
I'd rather hang around
The Picadilly Underground,
Living off the earnings of a high-born lady,
Don't want a bayonet up me arsehole,
Don't want me buttocks shot away![3]
I'd rather stay in England,
In merry, merry England,
And roger all me fuckin' life away,
Gorblimey!

Call out the Army and the Navy,
Call out the rank and file,
Call out the loyal Territorials,
They'll face danger with a smile,
Gorblimey!
Call out the members of the Old Brigade,
They'll set England free,
Call out your mother,
And your sister and your brother,
But for Christ's sake don't call me!

The reluctant warrior who does not want to risk injury or death in battle is a recurrent self-parody in Anglo-American occupational song. For instance, to the tune of "The Darktown Strutters' Ball," U.S. soldiers in World War 1 sang:

Machine gun bullets whizzing all around me,
Old tin hat feels mighty small,
Inside it I want to crawl
And hug the ground, just like a porous plaster,
My feet feel big and my knees feel weak,
I bite my tongue every time I speak,
And when the shells are dropping near,
I'm afraid I'm stopping here,
In No Man's Land where they play that shell-hole rag, Whizz-bang!
In No Man's Land where they play the shell-hole rag.[4]

"People Will Say We're at War" (to the tune of "People Will Say We're in Love") was sometimes whimsically sung by members of the 397th Infantry Regiment of the 100th U.S. Division "in a powerful monotone while shivering in a foxhole during World War 2."

Don't throw grenades at me,
Don't lob mortar shells,
Don't shoot your artillery,
People will say we're at war.

Don't throw grenades at me,
Don't pull that safety pin,
Kraut-buddy, don't you see,
People will say I'm done in.[5]

British and Commonwealth troops in World War 2 sometimes sang this chorus to the tune of the march "Our Director" (Hopkins* 1979).

We're a bunch of bastards,
Bastards are we!
We'd rather fuck than fight
For count-er-y!

Self-denigratory incompetence is the theme of "Fred Karno's Army" (Brophy and Partridge 1965; Cleveland 1959 and 1991; de Witt 1970; Nettleingham 1917) sung to the tune of "The Church's One Foundation." Fred Karno was an English music hall comedian during World War 1 who exploited the humorous possibilities of inefficiency and ineptitude. In World War 2, Hitler was substituted for the Kaiser.

We are Fred Karno's army,
The ragtime infantry,
We cannot fight, we cannot shoot,
No bloody use are we!
And when we get to Berlin
The Kaiser he will say,

Hoch! Hoch! Mein Gott!
What a bloody fine lot,
The ragtime infantry.

A variant of this song circulated in the Fleet Air Arm of the Royal Navy in World War 2 (Ward-Jackson 1967). The version below is reproduced from a leaflet compiled for the Dominion Conference of the Fleet Air Arm Association of New Zealand in Wellington, 1952.

We are the Air Sea Rescue,
No flaming use are we,
The only time you'll see us
Is breakfast, lunch and tea;
And when you're in your dinghy
By day or in the night,
Per adua ad astra,
Up you Jack, I'm all right!

Beneath the romantic ebullience and aggressive heroics of the songs of USAF pilots is a current of unease. A well-known World War 2 example is "I Wanted Wings" (Getz 1981 and 1986b*; Palmer 1944; Tuso 1990). A disillusioned warrior finds that when he gets his long sought-after qualification, he doesn't want it any more because "they teach you how to fly," then send you out to die. In a Korean War version reproduced by Getz, the disillusioned flier does not want his fanny frozen "in this putrid land of Chosin, fighting MIGs of Uncle Joe's."[6] A Vietnam War version is critical of the way the F-105 behaved "like 20 tons of grief" and devotes itself to a sobering discussion of the fate of prisoners of war and pilots who have been shot down in flames.

Since mechanical failure, accident or the inadequacy of aircraft and equipment are matters of life and death to aviators, their songs contain an understandable nervousness about the risks of flying. "You'll Never Mind" (Getz 1981) has been sung in World War 2, Korea and Vietnam by U.S. airmen. It canvasses some of the possibilities for engine failure or for being shot down, and then concludes that when you've been promoted and have got to the rank of general, you find the motors cough and your wings fall off, "but then you'll never mind!"

Another lyric entitled "Just Give Me Operations" (Getz 1981 and 1986a; Tuso 1971 and 1990) is an example of the importance attached to technology in this field of occupational song. It recites the mechanical defects of almost the entire range of aircraft in use in the USAF from World War 2 to Vietnam, beginning with the P-38 (or Lockheed Lightning), a World War 2, twin-engined fighter with props that tended to counterrotate and were "scattered and smitten from Burma to Britain."

The air war over Vietnam produced similar wry humor about the risks of combat flying. "Dodge City," sung by Dolf Droge, a U.S. Agency for International Development (USAID) officer in Vietnam with a considerable talent for improvising satirical and comic commentaries on events and personalities, summarized the feelings of naval pilots trying to avoid SAM missiles over Hanoi and hoping to rotate back to the United States "by and by."

> I don't want to get zapped over Dodge City,
> I don't want to get zapped in the sky,
> I wanna fly back to my aircraft carrier so pretty
> And rotate to the states by and by.
>
> Mechanics up all night with our aircraft they tinker,
> When that morning flak starts to rise,
> You better pull that stick back and you better jinker
> Or SAM missiles will make you de-materialize!
>
> Lady Bird Johnson wants to beautify America,
> I agree you see, I hope all those gunners in Hanoi
> Are really cross-eyed S.O.B.s,
> 'Cause I want to get America full of me (in one piece),
> I want to get America full of me.
>
> *Chorus:*
> I don't want etc.

Other songs joked about "hanging out your ass" on dangerous missions, about the capabilities of the MIG-21s flown by enemy pilots, the dangers of night flying ("the truth about my chances is they're not worth a dime"), the missions performed by rescue helicopters known as the "Jolly Green" and the services of "Puff the Magic Dragon" (see Lansdale* 1976; Tuso 1990). This was a helicopter gunship with tandem machine guns that had a very high rate of fire. It came "screaming from the sky" when the Grunts were "deep in trouble."

Pilots of the 48th Assault Helicopter Company held regular song sessions at their headquarters in Vietnam where, according to Broudy (1969), performances were given "in an active broadside tradition" that emphasized the peculiar skills as well as anxieties of their specialized occupation. For example, one item in the unit's songbook describes how they typically faced "the fear and danger of a chopper pilot's day."

A parody of "The Ballad of the Green Berets" included in Lansdale* (1976) has frightened soldiers dropping from the sky as they scream "Hell! I don't wanna die!" "Short Timers' Blues" in Broudy (1969) unashamedly confesses the anxiety of the draftee who is due to be rotated back to the homeland after 365 days of service. Short timers were those who had only a comparatively brief period of service to complete and who, understandably, wanted "to leave this country far behind" and felt "a yellow streak" creeping up their spines as they neared their completion dates.

The survival of the infantry soldier is not as elaborately and delicately related to the personal effort required to control complex machines like aircraft. It can often be thought of, more simply, as directly proportional to distance from the frontline. Those in the rear not only have a much more secure expectation of life, but also they can expect to enjoy comforts and pleasures denied the combat soldier. "South of the Sangro" (Hopkins 1979), sung to the tune of "South of the Border," satirizes those who found safety from the rigors of the Italian campaign in World War 2 among rear-echelon supply lines.

> South of the Sangro,
> Down Echelon way,
> That's where all the Wops
> And all the Quartermasters stay,
> A quiet night told me,
> It's better to stay,
> South of the Sangro
> Down Echelon way. Etc.

One's life expectancy in the infantry can be extended by such methods as feigning illness or insanity, malingering, going absent without leave or committing a crime serious enough to guarantee a court martial and a lengthy stay in a military prison. Another, less drastic method is to be left out of battle (LOB). Whenever an infantry company goes into an attack, it usually leaves its cooks, quartermaster staff and baggage party behind with its vehicles. This takes care of the company's spare equipment and ensures that a reservoir of people will be available for its reconstruction should those up front meet with total disaster. The LOB positions are often filled by soldiers who have seen long service or are encountering health problems that are not sufficiently disabling to hospitalize them. Lanning (1987:63) in his account of infantry warfare in Vietnam refers to those who have been left out of battle as REMFs ("rear-echelon mother fuckers"). Hopkins (1979) cites a Canadian World War 2 song, "When I am LOB," to the tune of "Lili Marlene" which celebrates the good fortune of a man in the rear areas who doesn't have to drag his feet through the mud as he listens to enemy weapons, gets on with the risky business of attacking the Wehrmacht and worries about Tiger tanks[7] in the vicinity of his slit trench.

Rationalizing defeat and joking about disaster are other important stratagems in the philosophy of reluctant endurance. G.I.s in World War 2 sang a parody of "Wedding Bells Are Breaking Up That Old Gang of Mine." This version from the Hamilton Collection is an acknowledgment of the deadly power of the German 88 mm field gun that dominated the battlefields of Europe.

> Oh I get that lonely feeling
> When I hear those fragments whine,
> Those 88s are breaking up
> That old gang of mine.[8]
>
> There goes Jack, there goes Jim
> Down through Sniper Lane;
> They'll come back to us some day,
> But they won't look the same.

"The Bug-out Ballad," sung to the tune of "Moving On" (Cray 1969 and 1992; Getz 1981) satirizes the precipitate retreat of the United Nations' forces from the Yalu River in Korea in 1950 when Chinese Communist troops came over the border.

> Hear the patter of a thousand feet,
> It's the First Cav in full retreat,
> They're movin' on,
> They'll soon be gone;
> They're haulin' ass,
> Not savin' gas,
> They're movin' on.

After an account of "a million Chinks coming through the pass/playing burp-gun boogie all over my ass," the song concludes:

> I'm movin' on,
> I'll soon be gone;
> I done my time
> In this shit and slime,
> I'm movin' on.[9]

"The Tennessee Cannonball," to the tune of "The Wabash Cannonball," describes the destruction of a U.S. armored column that ventured too aggressively into enemy terrain in World War 2. The Tennessee Cannonball tells his command that there's nothing up ahead, but 10 minutes later the whole task force is destroyed by German artillery fire. This salutary tale then concludes:

> So remember all you tankers
> As you burn that gasoline,
> Remember what the Colonel said

And what the Colonel's seen;
If you want to draw old-fogey pay
And see the folks next fall,
Stay 30 miles behind the tanks
Of the Tennessee Cannonball.[10]

Another World War 2 ballad, sung to the tune of "Down in the Valley," questions the disastrous consequences of obedience to the orders of "some chairborne General" when a promised fighter escort failed to arrive.

Down in Ruhr valley
Flying so low,
Some chairborne General
Says we must go.
Flak loves big bombers,
Fighters do too,
P-51 boys
What happened to you?
Send me a letter,
Send it to me,
Send it in care of
Stalag Luft Three.[11]

The reluctant warrior can demonstrate his fatigue and his nostalgia by singing about home and its attractions. "I Want to Go Home" is the title of a song that originated in the Boer War and was parodied in World War 1 and World War 2. This version is from the Cleveland Collection.

I want to go home,
I want to go home;
Of Mausers and Pompoms[12]
I've had quite enough
And the grub that they give us
Is so bloody tough;
Take me over the sea
Where the Boers can't get at me;
Oh my! I don't want to die!
I want to go home.

In the World War 1 version of this song,[13] the enemy becomes the German Army, and the weapons technology is updated to incorporate shrapnel fired by contemporary artillery. A copyright version with words and music by Lieutenant Gitz Rice (1st Canadian Contingent) was published in 1917, but by World War 2 its technical features had again become obsolescent, so Allied aviators amended the words to suit current German aircraft and weaponry. British and Commonwealth soldiers simply sang a very attenuated form of the original to the tune of the hymn "He Careth for Me."

> I want to go home,
> I want to go home,
> I'm sick of the army,
> I want to go home.[14]

The chief aim of the reluctant warrior is to get home, if possible, in one piece. A nineteenth-century ballad from the Spanish-American War expresses his determination to manage this, even if he is a battered wreck of skin and bones. The tune is a parody of "Sweet Marie."

> From the field of war I come, sweet Marie,
> Won't you kiss me welcome home, love, to thee;
> I am only skin and bones,
> All my sweetest songs are groans
> And I'm full of army prunes as can be.
>
> Oh I got it in the neck, sweet Marie,
> I am but a battered wreck, don't you see?
> In the mud and rain I slept
> While the very heavens wept,
> And the buzzards, vigil kept over me. Etc.[15]

U.S. troops in World War 1 used a comic parody deriving from the period of the Philippine insurrection (1890–1902) to remind them of the nostalgic attractions of home.

> Home boys, home, it's home we ought to be;
> Home boys, home, in the land of liberty;
> We'll nail Old Glory to the top of the pole
> And we'll all re-enlist, in a pig's asshole!
>
> Give us a barrel of whisky, sugar a hundred pound,
> A six-inch gun to mix it in, a spade to stir it round;
> We'll sit on the steps of the guardhouse
> And sing as we used to do,
> To hell with Aguinaldo and the WCTU.[16]

"When We Get Back Home Again," sung to the tune of "Bye, Bye, Blackbird," was equally unenthusiastic about the U.S. Navy in World War 2.

When we get back home again
We're not going USN,
Bye, bye, Navy;
This rotation plan is great,
It's never more than two years late,
Bye, bye, Navy.
No one in this outfit understands me,
Look at the scuttlebutt the Captain hands me;
Wings of gold and bars of brass,
You can shove them up your ass,
Navy goodbye![17]

In similar vein, "I Don't Want No More Army" (Loesser 1942; Lynn* 1961; Niles 1927; Palmer 1944; Posselt 1943) complains about the officers living on top of the hill, while the men who are obliged to subsist down in the slop and swill would like to go home.

For soldiers in Vietnam, the metaphor of "the World" symbolized the pleasures of home and the attractions of normal life in America. This was the more tantalizing because of the use of passenger jet aircraft to transport time-expired troops back to the United States. "Freedom Bird," a song by Bill Ellis (In Country* 1991; Lansdale* 1976) expresses a dreamlike yearning for the sound of the aircraft that will take the soldier home. One of the songs of the Utility Tactical Transport (Davis* 1987) uses the tune of "Sweet Chariot" to describe the emotions of those awaiting the arrival of a "sweet 707 coming for to carry me home."

Some services songs can be regarded as a kind of secular prayer because they either convey a plea for salvation from distress, or they make use of popular hymn tunes and religious lyrics like "Sweet Chariot" that are a familiar part of the homeland culture. In the England of World War 1, this was still embedded in an active tradition of Christian worship and an Evangelical movement that was a source of inspiration to believers and a comfort to the downtrodden and oppressed. This is why British soldiers in World War 1 were singing "When This Bloody War Is Over" (to the tune of "Take It to the Lord in Prayer"), "Raining, Raining, Raining" (to the tune of "Holy, Holy, Holy") and "We've Had No Beer" (to the tune of "Lead Kindly Light").[18]

In more recent times, the habit of formal religious worship and attendance may have lost much of its currency,[19] but among British and Commonwealth soldiers in World War 2 a repertoire of hymns like "He Careth for Me," "Take It to the Lord in Prayer," and "When the Roll Is Called Up Yonder" was a regular part of the brief, religious services that were held by the various welfare organizations in most base camps and training depots. Although some men were sustained by a personal religious faith, wore crosses and other religious emblems around their necks and attended church parades held by forces chaplains, the majority would never publicly express themselves in formal prayer. But hymn tunes, and the tradition of prayer, were part of the homeland popular culture that was a significant resource in the ordinary soldier's struggle to survive. Many ribald parodies contain direct echoes of the tradition of Christian prayer and belief in deliverance from evil. As lyrics rather than as mundane words, perhaps they signaled a degree of reassurance and even affirmation to those confronted by experiences and terrors for which no official explanation seemed adequate.

"The Soldier's Prayer" (Dallas 1972; Edwards* 1972b; Getz 1986a) is an example of this genre. It is a typical expression of the blasphemous anger of the powerless and has been current among British soldiers for at least 100 years. The combined-operations basis, involving a sailor and a soldier, and the abusive reference to "our Queen" suggest Victorian origins, perhaps during the Crimean campaign. However, it was still being sung in the following form in the N.Z. Division in 1943.[20] (See the Appendix for music.)

Oh a soldier and a sailor were talking one day;
Said the soldier to the sailor let us kneel down and pray,
And for each thing we pray for, may we also have ten
And at the end of every chorus we will both sing, Amen!

Now the first thing we'll pray for, we'll pray for some beer
And if we only get some it will bring us good cheer,
And if we have one beer, may we also have ten,
May we have a fucking brewery, said the sailor, Amen!

Now the next thing we'll pray for, we'll pray for some cunt,
And if we only get some it will make us all grunt,
And if we have one cunt, may we also have ten,
May we have a fucking knock shop, said the sailor, Amen!

Now the next thing we'll pray for, we'll pray for our Queen.
To us a bloody old bastard she's been,
And if she has one son, may she also have ten,
May she have a fucking regiment, said the sailor, Amen!

Now all you young officers and NCOs too,
With your hands in your pockets and fuck-all to do,
When you stand on street corners abusing us men,
May the Lord come down and fuck you all, said the sailor, Amen!

The combination of blasphemy, obscenity and antiauthoritarian invective gives this song a powerful and unique integrity, but the most widely known expression of dissident sentiment in World War 2 was probably "Fuck 'Em All." This was the ultimate in protest songs as well as being an example of the repetitive use of obscenity. The text reproduced here was current among New Zealand troops in the Pacific theater during World War 2.

> Oh they say there's a troopship just leaving Fiji,
> Bound for New Zealand's shore,
> Heavily laden with time-expired men,
> Bound for the land they adore;
> There's many a twat[21] just finishing his time,
> There's many a cunt signing on;
> You'll get no promotion
> This side of the ocean,
> So cheer up my lads, fuck 'em all!

Chorus:

> Fuck 'em all! Fuck 'em all!
> The long and the short and the tall,
> Fuck all the sergeants and W.O.ls,[22]
> Fuck all the corporals and their fucking sons;
> For we're saying goodbye to them all,
> As up the C.O.s[23] arse they crawl,
> You'll get no promotion
> This side of the ocean,
> So cheer up my lads
> Fuck 'em all!

The troops in Fiji usually appended a coda to the tune of the hymn "Blessed Assurance" (from the Cleveland Collection).

> This is my story, this is my song,
> We've been in the army too bloody long,
> Roll out the Rodney, salvage the Hood,
> For our Merchant Navy is no bloody good,
> Isa Lei, Isa Lei,[24]
> From Auckland to Cairo's a fucking long way!
> Isa Lei, Isa Lei,
> When I get to Auckland I'll fucking well stay.

Rodney was a battleship in the British Navy, and *Hood* was a battle cruiser. Troops returning to New Zealand in World War 2 had to make the journey by sea. The song suggests that if the merchant service couldn't do the job, perhaps the Navy could, even though *Hood* had been sunk in 1941.

Numerous adaptations of "Fuck 'Em All" circulated among U.S. troops in the Pacific theater in World War 2, including a Marine Corps version.[25]

> They called for the Army to come to Tulagi,
> But Douglas MacArthur said no,

And this is the reason,
It isn't the season,
Besides there's no USO.

Fuck 'em all! Fuck 'em all!
The long, the short, the tall;
Fuck all the admirals in ComSoPac,[26]
They don't give a shit if we never get back,
So we're saying goodbye to them all,
As over the gangplank we crawl,
There'll be no promotion
This side of the ocean
So cheer up my lads, fuck 'em all![27]

Another vehement dismissal of the entire apparatus of the services is contained in a World War 2 parody of "The Marines Hymn."[28]

Fuck the Army and the Navy,
Shove the Marine Corps up your ass;
I'm going back to civilian life
To sit on my big fat ass.

When the Army and the Navy
Look on Heaven's screens
They will fund that their wives
Are shacked up with United States Marines.

When the Army and the Navy
Sail out to meet the foe
You will find the brave U.S. Marines
In the nearest USO
A'drinkin' Namear.[29]

Another outlet for stress is in the recital of perilous combat incidents and adventures. Getz (1986a) cites "Tchepone" (also included in In Country* 1991). This is the story of an air raid on a North Vietnamese encampment astride the Ho Chi Minh Trail where the ground fire had a deadly intensity. Another well-known USAF example is "Itazuke Tower" (Fish 1989; Getz 1981 and 1986b*; Wallrich 1957) sung to the tune of "The Wabash Cannonball." This is the tale of a pilot whose plane blows up before he can get clearance to land. A variant from the Vietnam War known as "Hello Cam Ranh Tower" (Tuso 1971 and 1990) has the crippled aircraft crashing because a visiting VIP senator has been given landing priority. A feature of this and several more of the narratives in this song cycle is the dialogue between the despairing pilot in the failing aircraft and the uncaring or incompetent airfield controllers whose casual decisions determine the aviator's fate.

Other concerns in ballads collected by Broudy (1969), Tuso (1971 and 1990) and Getz (1981) deal with the problems of in-flight refueling, combat with the MIG-21 in Vietnam, the techniques of dodging SAM missiles and a variety of other operational hazards. Perhaps the reconstruction of fearful experience through the medium of narrative and song gives a broader cultural perspective that conveys greater understanding and meaning. This was certainly one of the payoffs from the recital of personal narratives in the platoon in which the writer served in World War 2.

The psychological condition of this organization in 1944–45 closely resembled the description of anxiety states given by Grinker and Spiegel (1945:14–16). It had been in action continuously since 1941 and had sustained repeatedly heavy losses, being almost completely destroyed on several occasions. There was no policy of rotation. A soldier posted to the platoon stayed there until he was either killed, wounded, taken prisoner, afflicted with sickness or directed to some other duties. Most men kept on fighting out of personal pride, a sense of commitment to the ideological objectives of the war and feelings of group loyalty to comrades. Under the stress of continuous operation, however, some of those who had survived more than about six months in action developed tremors of the limbs and other involuntary responses to battle sounds, had repetitive dreams in which they relived past crises, sometimes lost emotional control, on occasions of extreme stress appeared dazed and tear-stricken and whenever the opportunity presented itself, consumed large quantities of wine and other liquor to the point of stupefaction or insensibility.

Excessive drinking combined with communal singing sessions in the platoon were intuitive attempts at primitive self-therapy by which feelings of solidarity could be strengthened. Such techniques are not unlike some of the methods used by contemporary encounter groups in the attempt to lessen the anxieties associated with emotional problems and various states of bodily impairment including terminal illness. In the case of the platoon, however, the recognition of death, wounding and nervous stress was more obliquely expressed through symbolism, involuntary gesture and occasional song rather than by means of systematic discussion and other psychiatric procedures.

The use of song as therapy has parallels in other fields of occupational culture. For instance, Archie Green (1972) comments on the problem of accidental death and the industrial community's response to it. He speculates about the singing of "Only a Miner" in hotel bars after a man was killed. This song has many variants, but it is essentially a lament about the death of a young miner in an industrial mishap. Green thinks "these reports of group drinking and singing suggest that communal catharsis was one of the functions of this piece" (1972:19).

Sometimes in Italy, one of the singers in the platoon would give a performance of a very special song entitled "Castel Frentano" (Cleveland 1959, 1975*, 1982* and 1991*) with a degree of solemnity not otherwise evident in its vocal festivities. This was a lament that had been composed by an unknown source in the Maori Battalion and had been learned by some of the people in the platoon. It concerned events in the village of Castel Frentano during the Sangro River battles. The battalion suffered heavy losses in these actions, and even 12 months later, whenever the Sangro was mentioned, there were thoughtful silences and dour looks from the few survivors.

The village of Castel Frentano is on a hilltop that is crowned by a monastery. The singer hears its bells and fancies they are asking him where he is going. The audience, committed to an interminable and costly advance up the Italian peninsula, thinks of the fearful Sangro battles but declares that even so, they would sooner be there than in Milan to the north where the Nazis and Fascists are still in power.

The song (see Appendix) was always performed as a solo with dirgelike intensity by one particular soldier. Its solemnity, and the imagery of the fateful village and the dreaded Sangro River, were both an expression of grief for the dead and an intimation of concern for the future in the "many weary miles" and the mud, terror, cold and exhaustion of an interminable campaign. The concluding acceptance of this future as a matter of preference was a gratifying collective dramatization of the audience's situation. It proclaimed a conventional, warriorlike fidelity to the common cause that placed them in the socially approved context of the general crusade against fascism, whatever their private misgivings might have been.

When not sustained by such collective heroics, the individual soldier can always engage in the kind of imaginative, personal therapy by which thoughts can be directed away from the subject of anxiety (nearby gunfire, a patrol duty, the next attack and so on) toward an internal universe of private distraction. For instance, in the infantry battalions of the N.Z. Division it was possible, in the final stages of the Italian campaign, for an ordinary soldier to cultivate a degree of alternative identity as a private personality with distinctive and sometimes idiosyncratic characteristics. This was symbolized by a relaxation (when out of the frontline and not engaged in formal duties) of dress standards that enabled decorative varieties of nonregulation attire to be worn.

A strange variety of civilian hats made their appearance, and some warriors affected bright red scarves worn around the neck in the style of an Italian partisan, while others sported walking sticks. This demonstration of personal autonomy was a reminder of linkages with an alternative civilian culture. It also served to distinguish the wearer as a combat soldier who was not quite so subservient to the disciplinary standards imposed on his rear-echelon cohorts. Sossamen (1989:76) has described a similar material statement of individual identities by the personalization of uniforms, in the case of U.S. troops in the Vietnam War. He noted that it was tolerated in proportion to the soldier's involvement in combat. Such scope for deviation from official standards by the cultivation of personal space may be a general cultural trait of democratic armies in wartime.

Another way of distancing oneself from a tiresome or repugnant situation is to engage in daydreaming, fantasy and childish play. For example, a New Zealand infantry soldier in World War 2 used to perform a curious dance that he called "Unlucky for Some" in the course of periodic revels in his company lines. In this dance he parodied and mimed the actions of infantry committed to the demanding procedures of a frontal attack with a supporting barrage. The name of the dance is inspired by the game of Housie (or Bingo) in which the number 13 can be called as "Unlucky for Some."

Frequently, whole groups of carousing New Zealand soldiers, on impulse, and still shouting and singing, would form themselves into an impromptu rugby football scrimmage in which they would thrust and push against each other in the pursuit of either an imaginary football or some convenient surrogate item of equipment, apparel or furniture. Such scrimmages offered the comforting possibility of close body contact for a socially legitimate purpose and fulfilled some of the functions of dance by enriching the opportunities for self-expression and imaginative escape from an oppressive and fearful environment.

Alternatively, the scrimmage could be seen as a replay of a childish game called "Stacks on the Mill" in which everyone just piled on top of each other to the chant of "stacks on the mill, more on still." Perhaps as a game it also symbolized the war itself—a crude contest between two teams in which some ended up as winners and others as losers.

One expressive function of dance described by Langer (1953:20) is to provide entry to an infantile world of spontaneous, irresponsible reactions and wish-potency freedom. During the Gulf War, U.S. Marines stationed at a supply base near the Kuwait border were reported to be using computerized rap music in their disco recreation tent and were "attempting to take their minds off everything going on outside" by performing the "Gasmask Dance" in which "you put your hands to your face, simulate panic, then stomp your feet."[30]

Childlike memories can also be indulged with nursery rhyme jingles like "Little Miss Muffet" (Cleveland 1961*). This song was sung on the march in 4/4 time by British and Commonwealth soldiers in World War 1 and World War 2 (from the Cleveland Collection).

Little Miss Muffet, Muffet,
Sat on a tuffet, tuffet,

Eating her curds and whey,
Whey! Whey! Whey! Whey!
Along came a spider, spider,
Sat down beside her, side her,
Frightened Miss Muffet away
Way! Way! Way! Way!

Star of the Evening,
Beautiful Star!
Star of the evening,
Shining on the shithouse door!

Or like "Mrs. Porter" sung to the tune of "Pretty Redwing."

The moon shines bright on Mrs. Porter
And on her daughter, her lovely daughter;
She washes her feet in soda water,
And so she oughter to keep them clean.

The favorite lyric of the 351st Infantry, 88th Division in the AEF, 1917–19, was an adaptation of the chorus of Stephen Foster's "Old Dog Tray."

Old dog Tray was ever faithful,
Gr-ief couldn't drive him away.
Way! Way! Way! Way!
He was faithful he was ki-yind
And you'll never, never fi-yind
Another dog like
Old dog Tray etc. (repeated *ad infinitum*)[31]

The nostalgic consolations of the reluctant warrior also include the occasional performance of well-known nonsense rhymes. In World War 2, U.S. soldiers sang "My Gal's a Corker" (Getz 1986a) and "Midnight on the Ocean," which is the scene for an encounter with a lady "old and grey" who used to peddle shoestrings on the road to Mandalay.[32]

NOTES

1. One of them is in a manuscript in the World War 2 subject file in the Archive of Folk Culture at the Library of Congress. This is transcribed from recordings made by a group of singers in the 1st Raider Battalion, 1st Marine Raider Regiment at Noumea, New Caledonia, 1943. Other versions are located in Brophy and Partridge 1965; Cleveland 1959; Cray 1992*; de Witt 1970; Getz 1986a; Glazer* 1970; Hart* 1971; Hopkins* 1979; Lynn* 1961; Nettleingham 1917; Page 1973. The alternative title, "The Picadilly Song," is derived from the reluctant warrior's preference for hanging about Picadilly Underground, a no-

torious wartime venue for prostitutes. The payment of seven shillings and six-pence per week would be the result of a magistrate's order for the maintenance of an illegitimate child.

2. The performance is by a group of USAF entertainers called the Merrymen who, for the occasion, try to simulate pseudo-British accents. Getz (1986a) lists seven variants current in the USAF. The Merrymen's source could have been this tradition.

3. Rathbone (1979:313–14) reproduces an earlier text in which the warrior prefers to live off "the pickings of the Ladies of the Town" and doesn't want his "cobblers minced with ball" (i.e., his testicles injured by a shot from a musket or cannon), but if he has to lose them he would rather it be "with Susan, or Peg or Meg, or any whore at all!"

4. Gordon Collection, LC. See also Dolph (1929).

5. Hamilton Collection.

6. The Chosin Reservoir was a position on the Korean front near the Chinese border. It was the scene of heavy fighting when a Communist offensive began on 26 November 1950 and the Ist Marine Division was outflanked. The MIG was a Russian fighter used by the Communists. Uncle Joe was a World War 2 sobriquet for Marshal Stalin.

7. According to Hopkins (1979), this song was composed by four officers of the Loyal Edmonton Regiment (Major James "Big Jim" Stone, Lieutenant "Duke" Kitching, Lieutenant W. Remple and Lieutenant Owen R. Browne).

> When you hear the Tigers grinding by your slit,
> Makes you start to wonder if it's time to quit,
> Just think of me in Gay Paree,
> With some French wench upon my knee,
> For I am LOB, for I am LOB.

The Tiger Tank was the general Anglo-American designation in World War 2 for the German Pz.Kw.VI tank. It weighed 56 tons, carried an 88 mm gun that fired a high-velocity shell and had very heavy armor plate on its superstructure, front and turret mantlet. It was immune to British and American antitank weapons except at very short range, and its front was immune to the 75-pounder gun on the Sherman tanks used by the Allied armies. Most Allied infantry were scared of the Tiger Tank as they were of the versatile 88 mm gun. Originally designed as an antiaircraft weapon, it was mounted on four wheels and could be used either as a field artillery piece, as an antitank gun or in its antiaircraft role. It fired a 20.25 pound shell up to a height of 35,000 feet or to a distance of 16,200 yards on the ground. It could penetrate 99 mm of armor at 2,200 yards.

8. A Korean War version collected in 1950 has mortar shells breaking up that old gang of mine.

9. A New Zealand variant has two kinds of man the First Cavalry can't stand: "A North Korean and a Chinaman. They're movin' on, they're movin' on" and so forth. A Vietnam War version has a convoy flying through Man Giang Pass "playing the Purple Heart Boogie on the Air Cav's ass, I'm movin' on" etc.

10. Indiana.

11. Berkeley. See also Getz 1981; Wallrich 1957.

12. The Mauser rifle was the standard infantry weapon used by the Boers in the Boer War and subsequently by Germany in World War 1 and World War 2. A Pompom was a type of heavy machine gun, now obsolete, which had a bore of about 1 inch.

13. See Brophy and Partridge 1965; Nettleingham 1917; Palmer* 1944; Peat and Smith* 1932; Ward-Jackson 1967; York 1931.

14. Familiar to the troops through its use in brief, interdenominational services held in Salvation Army canteens.

15. Western Kentucky (Wilgus Collection).

16. Gordon "Inferno" LC, c. 1927. Aguinaldo was the leader of the insurrection. WCTU is the Women's Christian Temperance Union.

17. Indiana. Collected in 1955.

18. See Brophy and Partridge (1965) for a treatment of these and other songs sung on the march in World War 1.

19. But the power of inspirational song remains. For instance, a North African folksong, "All My Trials Lord," popularized by Peter, Paul and Mary, was current among U.S. troops in Vietnam. It had special significance to those who were counting the days before rotation.

20. Two 1909 versions are noted by Sharpe (1914). He considers it an adaptation of a much older ballad, "The Mare and the Foal" (see Karpeles 1974:363). The Edwards version was collected from an informant whose uncle learned it when he was in the British Army in India "around the turn of the century."

21. Slang for the female genitals or "cunt," hence in the sexist imagery of a male-dominant military culture, a foolish, silly, stupid or sometimes nasty person.

22. Warrant officers, first class.

23. The C.O. is the commanding officer.

24. "Isa Lei" is the title of a popular Fijian farewell song known to all who served in Fiji. The coda is an adaptation of part of a Royal Air Force troopship song entitled "Shire, Shire, Somersetshire." According to Ward-Jackson (1945), this originated in Iraq while the RAF was stationed there. The S.S. *Somersetshire* was an RAF troopship. Ward-Jackson (1945) also explains that "Bless 'Em All" originated in the Royal Naval Air Service (the progenitor of the RAF) in 1916. Subsequently, it became the unofficial RAF trooping song.

25. Located in the World War 2 subject file in the Archive of Folk Culture at the Library of Congress. Alternatively, "Fuck all the Pelicans and Dogfaces too." Dogface is slang for the U.S. infantry soldier. According to Palmer (1944:187), Pelicans are medical corps personnel.

26. ComSoPac was the wartime South Pacific Command.

27. Alternatively, "On MacArthur's blue ocean/So cheer up Gyrenes, fuck 'em all!" This is an allusion to the domineering aspects of the personality of General Douglas MacArthur, commander of the South-west Pacific area in World War 2. Gyrenes is slang for U.S. Marines.

28. Indiana. Collected in 1950.

29. The brand name of a southern beer.

30. The *Evening Post*, Wellington, New Zealand, 7 February 1991.

31. Hamilton Collection. The informant stated that he had heard a thousand men sing it by the hour.

32. Indiana.

4

The Bawdy Warrior

When the warrior is not indulging in mordant humor about his situation, he may be venting his sadistic alarm in violent sexuality. Songs like "Little Angeline" (Getz 1986a); "Carolina the Cowpuncher's Whore" (Cray 1992*; Getz 1986a); "Kafoozalem" (Brand* 1960; Cray 1969 and 1992*; Getz 1986a; Hopkins* 1979; McGregor 1972; Silverman* 1982) and "Rangy Lil" (Getz 1986a) deal in feats of sadistic coitus by what Getz describes as "macho man matching his sexual prowess against a super-sexy woman."

Perhaps the most notorious example of this genre is "Lupee" (sung to the tune of "Down in the Valley" and located in Cray 1969 and 1992*; Getz 1986a). She is involved in a sexual intercourse contest with a "lanky Texan" who has a 17-inch penis! However, the song can also be seen as an example of what Legman (1978:803–29) calls antigallantry, a part of a long-standing conflict between men and women. It is also a racial insult. Lupee is described as a "Mexican whore," and the smile on her face is "a mute cry for more." Such male fantasies about violent sex are displacements of sadistic anger that help relieve the anxieties of combat or any other source of traumatic stress. As expressions of deviancy from conventional, middle-class standards of morality, they may also contribute to the cohesion of male groups by exploiting the sense of participation in forbidden or socially taboo activity.

Cray points out the importance of the comic element in bawdy songs (1992:xxxii). Those that are not funny are not memorable. When the present writer's platoon sang "O'Reilly's Bar" in the course of drinking sessions during World War 2, they enjoyed the savage, childlike humor of the balled in which the heavy father is outwitted with violent sadism and his daughter is triumphantly possessed. Tunes are another source of expressive pleasure in the repertoire of bawdiness. "O'Reilly's Bar" has a vigorous, assertive rhythm and a boisterous chorus constructed from a curious medley of ribald images that can be shouted out fortissimo after each verse.

> Oh, as I was sitting in O'Reilly's Bar
> Drinking O'Reilly's rum and water,
> Suddenly a thought came into my head
> That I would up O'Reilly's daughter.
>
> *Chorus:*
>
> Iddy-aye-ay, iddy-aye-ay
> Iddy-aye-ay for the One-eyed O'Reilly,
> Rub-a-dub-dub, balls and all,
> Jig-a-jig-jig, tray bong!
>
> So up the stairs and into bed,
> First I got the right leg over,
> Never a word the maiden said,
> But she laughed like hell when the fun was over.
>
> Iddy-aye-ay etc.
>
> Heard a footstep on the stairs,
> Who should it be but the One-eyed O'Reilly,
> Pair of pistols in his hand,
> Looking for the one who upped his daughter.
>
> Iddy-aye-ay etc.
>
> Grabbed O'Reilly by the balls,
> Jammed his head in a pail of water,
> Rammed his pistols up his arse,
> Bloody sight harder than I upped his daughter.
>
> Iddy-aye-ay etc.

Cray (1992:xv) notes a decline in the number of bawdy songs currently in the oral tradition in America. He attributes this change to a reduction in self-entertainment owing to the increased use of the electronic media, the waning of the urban folk music revival of the 1950–60s and the sexual revolution which has made sexual activity less inhibited. However, the bawdy warrior's need for distraction, self-therapy and self-entertainment suggests that the military services might have now become the major custodians of this particular canon.

Many of the bawdy songs and rhymes that circulate in the military are exercises in imaginative liberation from boring, repetitive situations that can be varied by fantasizing. Here the erotic regions of folklore lend themselves to exploration by male subcultures temporarily enduring periods of sexual deprivation. The most famous of all World War 1 soldiers' songs, "Madamoiselle from Armentieres," is a fantasy about a sexual assault on a helpless young Frenchwoman with "lily-white breasts and flaxen hair." The uninhibited environments of two world wars allowed the open expression of twentieth-century sexual folklore, revolving around a constellation of the erotic female stereotypes noted in Cleveland (1985) and encouraged by male fantasies concerning the sexual possession and dominance of women.

Nor is it any surprise that some of the cadences circulating in the training camps of the U.S. armed services have variants that are exercises in erotic fantasy. For instance, the alleged sexual proclivities of the women of various cities are the subject of innumerable rhyming couplets in this vein.

> I've got a girl in Kansas City,
> She's got freckles on her titties;
> Move that company and move it fast,
> Company B is on your ass;
> I've got a girl in Louisville,
> She won't do it but her sister will.[1]

The erotic imagination has no boundaries. It is the inspiration for a girl-in-every-port conceit entitled "The Girls I Met."[2] An amorous sailor recalls "Sweet Marie from Gay Paree," "Rita from Rome" and the "dusky queens of the Philippines" before he is "anchored for life with a cute little wife" back in the United States. The providential discovery of a whorehouse with an obliging staff in attendance is the subject of an erotic fantasy entitled "Far Across the Ocean," sung to the tune of "Philippino Baby."[3] In this song the soldier dreams of being received by "a lovely half-dressed whore," only to experience a sordid awakening in his own bunk.

Troops in the Middle East theater during World War 2 were both appalled and fascinated in Egypt. On the one hand, many were disgusted by the poverty, disease and misery of the bulk of the peasantry, but on the other hand, some were impressed by the great wealth and privilege possessed by the ruling classes. They saw Farida (then queen of Egypt) as a glittering symbol of sexuality who was being badly treated by the corrupt, overweight King Farouk. Sung widely throughout the British Army, "King Farouk" (to the tune of "Salaam el Malik," the Egyptian national anthem) expressed their typical reactions toward an inequitable regime at the same time as it indulged the sexual fantasies of a male subculture excited by the glamorous trappings of female royalty. On this question Mick Shepherd comments that

The youthful, shapely and attractive Farida was depicted as being wholly subservient to the despot. She could thus be taken to represent the 95 percent of the population who owned practically nothing in the material sense and who had no hope of improving their station in life. Of course, in point of fact, Farida obviously led a free lifestyle. She wore Western clothing and was quite often seen being driven about in her car or visiting some of the larger shops. Newspapers would mention her presence at functions or social gatherings, and no one could have been unaware of these activities.[4]

> Oh we're all black bastards
> And we all love our King,
> *Stanna shwya, kwise kateer,*
> *Mungarya bardin.*[5]

> Old King Farouk
> Put Farida up the chute[6]
> *Stanna shwya,* pull your wire,[7]
> King Farouk, *bardin.*

> Queen Farida, Queen Farida.
> All the boys want to ride her.
> But they never get a chance
> Their ambition to enhance;
> *Stanna shwya,* pull your wire,
> King Farouk, *bardin.*

An alternative version collected by Shepherd describes Farouk as a big, black brute[8] who gets Farida pregnant and then goes philandering. Henderson (c.1945) cites a version that refers to Farouk's pro-Axis leanings.[9]

Songs with a libidinous content circulating informally among troops in World War 2 were a vulgar counterpoint to the erotic popular art with which they were regaled in officially approved pin-ups and comic strips. These featured the wholesome attractions of Rita Hayworth, Betty Grable and other idealized surrogates for the girl back home. As sex objects, these were thought to strengthen morale by reminding the warrior of what was supposed to be worth fighting for. Milton Caniff, creator of a syndicated strip called "Terry and the Pirates," also supplied material free of charge for U.S. services newspapers. This included a strip called "Male Call" that featured Miss Lace, a demure but voluptuous brunette who was involved in an endless series of potentially amorous situations with G.I.s.

British servicemen were treated to "Jane," a *Daily Mirror* strip drawn by Norman Pett. She was a blue-eyed blonde who, unlike Miss Lace, was unable to keep her clothes on. In each installment, she either lost her underwear or was discovered removing it. Her nude, shapely figure was said to be worth at least two armored divisions. Perhaps the ultimate sexual fantasy of World War 2 was the depiction of sexual intercourse with an aircraft. In Getz (1981) the pilot envisages "her" stripped and bare, gets inside her, handles her gently, rolls her over, tries her on her back and decides that "she was just one high thrill, the best in the land, the P-51 of the Fighter Command."[10]

Not all fantasies reach such exotic extremities. For instance, combat experiences can be dramatized as tall-tales and epic accomplishments. The following extract from an interview with a Vietnam veteran recalls how his buddy used to make up stories about himself and "his rusty old M-16." Thompson (1955) cites a talking sword, a magic gun that is always loaded and an infallible firearm that never misses, but one of the problems with automatic weapons under jungle conditions is to keep them clean enough for instant use. A weapon that is self-cleaning and that announces when it is ready for renewed action is a contemporary, high-technology variant of these ancient motifs. It also invites analysis as a type of humorous exaggeration that depends on telling lies about a professional or an occupational skill.

"There I stood with a cliff to my back and my rusty M-16, pulling the pins out of grenades with my teeth. Grenades in one hand and my rusty M-16 in the other hand. And my rusty M-16 ceases to fire. I throw the rusty M-16 down and say, Clean! My rusty M-16 jumps up and says, Clean! I load my rusty M-16 up and start firing. Automatically I continue to throw grenades. Pull pins with my teeth. Throw grenades with my right and fire with my left hand." He just made it up you know, while he was over there. Like he was a big hero, like he was John Wayne or something.[11]

In 1984 a Vietnam veteran was circulating a comic-strip version of "The Island of the Black Clap." This legend describes an incurable type of venereal disease. Those who caught it were said to have been exiled to a Pacific island or put aboard a hospital ship that remained forever at sea. Another legend that circulated in Vietnam was one to the effect that some Vietnamese prostitutes had a method of secreting razor blades in their vaginas in such a way that when a soldier had intercourse with them his penis was sliced to shreds. This was said to be because they hated Americans and/or were secret agents of the Vietcong.

Whether these legends were the product of the G.I. imagination, or whether they were fabrications by the Military Assistance Command (MACV) intended to discourage troops from patronizing brothels and engaging in sexual intercourse is unclear. In the latter event it would have had some resemblance to Allied, officially inspired rumors in North Italy in 1944 to the effect that the retreating Germans had deliberately infected prostitutes with V.D. in the towns they evacuated. The object of this campaign was to discourage soldiers from sexual intercourse with the civilian population because the V.D. rate was already a serious problem in some formations and it was feared it might get worse.

Some legends are encouraged by military commands in the expectation that they will nurture feelings of espirit de corps. For instance, St. Barbara continues to be venerated as the patron saint of artillerymen, even though she was decanonized in 1969. A brief history of the life of the saint, distributed by the U.S. Seventh Field Artillery Association in 1969, explains that when gunpowder made its appearance in the Western world she was invoked for aid against the tendency of early artillery pieces to blow up. An Order of St. Barbara medallion can be worn at U.S. Field Artillery official functions such as St. Barbara's Day celebrations, field artillery balls and dinners. In New Zealand, a handbook distributed to all gunners of the Royal Regiment of New Zealand Artillery contains an account of the saint's legendary origins and claims that as the patroness of fire, cannon and firearms, she can also be invoked against the thunder and lightnings of Heaven. Her feast day on 4 December is celebrated by the regiment each year.

Two nuclear weapons were said to have been stored in the Long Binh ammunition dump in Vietnam,[12] but this rumor may have been inspired by the fact that a small, secret group had been established by MACV to study the possibility of using tactical nuclear weapons against the enemy at the siege of Khe Sanh in 1968 (Westmoreland 1976:444).

Another widespread legend claimed that a white American G.I. had been seen in the ranks of the Vietcong, fighting for the Communist cause. This achieved musical expression in "The Ballad of the Unknown Soldier" (Dallas* 1972), a popular song that circulated among the antiwar movement, about a young G.I. who dies heroically in the Mekong Delta wearing black pajamas, sandal-clad and rifle in hand.

If the inventive fields of narrative and legend are insufficient to divert the anxieties of the apprehensive warrior, then perhaps their source can be wrenched into an ironically diminished perspective by satirizing it, belittling it or making it the target for derisive or scatological humor. For instance, enemies can be psychologically reduced by investing them with ludicrous and demeaning imagery. In World War 1 the German command was the butt of a stream of caricatures and lampoons satirizing their capacities as war leaders. A scurrilous song entitled "Chamber Lye" (sung to the tune of "O Tannenbaum") labeled Field Marshal Paul Von Hindenburg (chief of the German General Staff) as "a funny creature" for allegedly sending barrels around town in which to gather up quantities of female urine in order to have it manufactured into nitre, an essential ingredient in gunpowder. The song is a variant of a composition that circulated in the Spanish-American War,[13] which describes how the

Dorothy Wenzel, a singer in USO Troupe 975, performing for a 25th Infantry Division audience during a rainstorm in Korea, May 1951. *(National Archives)*

A soldier in the U.S. 25th Infantry Division in Korea, December 1951, reading a pictorial magazine. *(National Archives)*

A wartime collection of pin-ups in a barracks at Greenville, South Carolina, July 1943. Such displays, as well as wartime declarations of amorous enthusiasm for female stars and entertainers are "social affirmations of virility" (Costello 1985:192). *(Library of Congress)*

Graffiti on the wall of a billet in Mersah Matruh, Egypt, December 1941. *(R.A. McDougall Collection, Alexander Turnbull Library, Wellington, New Zealand)*

Ray Milland and two female entertainers in his USO Camp Show Troupe visiting soldiers on Espiritu Santo, Pacific Theater, March 1944. *(National Archives)*

Reproduced by courtesy of W. T. "Tuck" Boys, manager of Bien Hoah Productions, Fayetteville, Arkansas.

ladies of Manila were asked by the Ordnance Department to preserve their chamber lye for collection "in the cause of Spain." Cray (1969:140–41) cites Gershon Legman, an authority on bawdy songs, to the effect that Von Hindenburg is a descendant of John Haroldson of the American Civil War when "Southern womanhood were asked to do their bit for the bonnie blue flag by saving urine."

In World War 2, Hitler and the Nazi leadership succeeded the Kaiser and Von Hindenburg as targets for the satiric attentions of the popular culture. A favorite marching song of British and Commonwealth troops (to the tune of "Colonel Bogey") claimed that the Nazi leadership was sexually abnormal (Hopkins 1979; Silverman 1982).

> Hitler has only got one ball,
> Goering has two but very small,
> Himmler has something similar,
> But poor old Goebbels has no balls at all!

Some narratives take the form of mock prayers that are a vehicle for criticism and complaint. "The Paratrooper's Prayer"[14] originated in 1940 at Fort Benning, Georgia, and has become part of the folklore of U.S. Airborne formations. It complains about the red tape emanating from Washington, D.C., the rates of pay and the military police who, it claims, were recruited from those who failed jump school.

Our Almighty Father who dwelleth in Washington immersed in service records, requisitions, T.S. slips, red tape and other impediments which surroundeth the Army both in time of peace and time of war, hallowed be thy Name. Give us this day our Partial Pay and forgive us our company bills. Guide us on the path of Righteousness by the all-knowing Articles of the War and Rules and Regulations. Approve our passes and furloughs, for thou knowest ours is not an easy lot to bear without leisure time. Deliver us from the hands of non-jumping Military Police, for thou knowest our burdens are manifold. . . .

The prayer asks for protection from accidents with static lines and break cords and prays that trainees will be drifted clear of Cactus Hill. It seeks guidance in the "lower regions of sin and iniquity known locally as Phoenix City lest we should go astray and contract certain Social uncleanliness which thou so forcefully describeth in thy Sex Hygiene Training Film."

Military life can be visualized as a violent fantasy. This treatment has the merit of obscuring its oppressive realities by imposing a different kind of order on people and events so that the warrior assumes a triumphant, anarchic potency. In songs like "The Cavalry" and "Colonel Pearson's Troopers"[15] the singers assert their aggressive identity with a frantic zest.

> Bing, bang, gosh dang, who the hell are we?
> Ida-mighty, gosh-almighty, we're the cavalry!
> We're going after Hitler mighty hard and fast,
> We're going to stick a bayonet right up his ass;
> Ida-mighty, gosh-almighty, we're the Cavalry!

and

> We're Colonel Pearson's troopers,
> The rapers of the night,
> We're dirty sons of bitches,
> We'd rather fuck than fight;
>
> Oh hi-dee, di-dee, Christ Almighty!
> Who the hell are we?
> Wham! Bam! God damn!
> The parachute infantry!

The preference for sexual intercourse rather than battle connects the latter song to "The Midnight Fusiliers." This work has eighteenth-century origins and was sung in British and Commonwealth armies at least until World War 2. It was certainly performed among the AEF in France during 1917–18. One informant relates how the song was generally used after a period of extreme fatigue or exasperation had irritated everyone, for instance, when his unit, the Sixth Machine Gun Battalion, U.S. Marines, had been on the march for 18 hours on less than half rations. It was a provocative piece that by tacit understanding was saved for very special occasions. It had a soothing effect that probably diverted the men from more or less rash acts of a mutinous type.[16] (See Appendix for music.)

> Eyes right! Foreskins tight!
> Assholes to the front!
> We're the boys who make no noise
> We're always after cunt!
> We're the heroes of the night
> And we'd rather fuck than fight,
> We're the buddies of the Skinback Grenadiers
> And the glory of the Midnight Fusiliers. Etc.

The ultimate, nihilistic rejection of all authority and all the complexities of circumstance that conspire to harass the life of the ordinary soldier is contained in the simple expletive "Fuck 'Em!" Legman (1964:389) suggests that this and similar obscenities may perhaps be founded in superstitious beliefs about the advisability of turning away a compliment with a deprecatory remark that might serve to ward off the evil eye. Alternatively, they may be thought of simply as being in conformity with a style of popular humor that automatically depicts the world in wry, ironic, devalued terms.

Expressions like "fuck you," "go fuck yourself," "get fucked," "fuck off" and "fucking" used as an adjectival modifier are derogatory usages employed by some soldiers to deride or diminish anything of a serious nature said by anybody. In this way the dangerous potentialities of a situation, a person or some threatening object can be symbolically reduced. Perhaps the repetition of the word is also a reminder of an alternative life of erotic pleasures that are not immediately available.

The hope that dangers can be averted and risks reduced by appropriate procedures is implicit in all military preparations, including the carrying of talismans and good luck charms, the naming of weapons, aircraft, vehicles and ships in affectionate, romantic and easily identifiable terms, along with the performance of the kind of precombat rituals described by Underwood (1947) in the hope that "correct, carefully planned behavior would avert misfortune." Wallrich (1960) cites the example of a co-pilot in Korea who refused to take off until he had urinated on the nose-wheel of his aircraft. In World War 2, most pilots carried lucky objects, and almost every air gunner had a picture of his girl friend, a Hollywood star or his mother pinned up in his turret. Baby shoes were popular, as were items of female underwear (Wallrich 1960). Some airmen thought it unlucky ever to say goodbye, and many U.S. pilots thought that it was bad luck to wear G.I. wings and that it was better they should be entrusted to the owner's wife, girl friend or mother. A pilot in the Burma theater carried a miniature rolling pin which his wife had given him to remind him that she was waiting at home. "I think a lot of the fellows had little things like that from wives and sweethearts that they liked to pretend kept them immune from ghoulies and danger, though I never saw anyone go back to the area just before a flight because he'd forgotten Polly's powder puff," stated an informant.[17]

In World War 2, plenty of people carried photos of girl friends and wives, and a few had St. Christopher medallions attached to a belt loop or a button hole. In the writer's platoon, it was universally believed that some men bore a mysterious immunity from harm. One very experienced soldier who had come right through the Italian campaign without a scratch was believed to be so lucky that anyone who stuck closely to him in an attack would also be spared.

The literature of the Vietnam War contains many examples of men who were obsessively attached to T-shirts, hats, teddy bears, beads and other adornments as well as particular aircraft that were believed to be luckier than others. In addition to believing in superstitious precautions, calling a defective computer or a broken-down tank a "useless fucker" or a "stupid mother-fucker" is to humanize its mechanical abstraction and to encourage at least the illusion that it has been brought under some kind of personal control. The violent obscenity of such utterances also gives vent to feelings of anger and anxiety. The moving thread that runs through all such expressive behavior is the presentation of life as an ironic, superstitious and violently savage fantasy.

Crude humor, obscenity and fantasy should not be seen as exclusive to democratic armies. For example, a notebook kept by Helmut Metzner, a Wehrmacht soldier in 164 Light Infantry Division, was found by Mick Shepherd in a satchel near the dead man's body in Tunisia on 21 March 1943. It contained a collection of poems, songs, recitations and jokes, some of which confirm that the ordinary World War 2 German soldier had much the same access as his Allied counterparts to an unofficial popular culture with possibilities for indulgence in erotic fantasy.

A bawdy parody of "Lili Marlene" concludes with the singer imagining himself having sexual intercourse with her, "all bliss and desire," only to see her next look around for a replacement (*ersatz*, a subject for much wise-cracking in wartime Germany) when he is no longer able to satisfy her. The notebook details the sexual exploits of "Hot Blooded Hilda" and Frau Wirtin, two figures of erotic fantasy, roughly the equivalent in popular German folklore of Tiger Lily, Eskimo Nell, Salome, Charlotte the Harlot, Lulu the Zulu, the Winnipeg Whore and the like. It also describes the various stages of sexual passion in terms of Nazi party slogans like Triumph of the Will and Strength Through Joy, while the shifting fashions of love are traversed month by month in "Monatsgedicht."

The Wehrmacht military culture appears to have had its frustrated sexuality and even mild jokes about the political regime, but to have sustained nothing with the nihilistic power of "Fuck 'Em All!" Perhaps in symbolic terms this was what World War 2 was all about—the democratic right to sing or say what one liked and to assert healthy attitudes of contempt, ridicule, indifference, personal resistance and even hatred toward authority as a way of taking some sturdy precautions to preserve one's survival as an individual person. From this perspective, the occupational culture of the military services contains a wide-ranging expressive repertoire that ranges from compliance with the military system to extreme opposition to it. On the one hand, it contributes to the official values that military organizations promote and feature in their integrative rituals, ceremonies, uniforms, insignia, specialized jargon, narratives, cadence calls and the occupational songs of the happy warrior. On the other hand, it offers large possibilities for indulgence in erotic fantasy as well as protest, opposition and grumbling.

NOTES

1. Western Kentucky. Collected in 1975.
2. Gordon Collection, 1924, LC.

3. Western Kentucky.

4. Shepherd to Cleveland, 24 July 1980.

5. Arabic nonsense, which translated literally means: "wait, very nice, food later." It is also an example of the complex argot spoken by Eighth Army troops in the Middle East.

6. Slang: "King Farouk has got Farida pregnant." This is a sexual fantasy involving the voluptuous Farida.

7. Slang: "masturbate."

8. A reference to Farouk's gross physique. The disparaging terms in which he is described here place this song in the medieval tradition of flyting or "contests-in-insult."

9. Farouk's tendency to listen to pro-Axis factions in Egyptian politics culminated in a battery of British artillery being trained on his palace at the height of the German threat to the Middle East. Shepherd claims (correspondence, 14 July 1976) that, in contrast to Farouk, Farida was generally regarded by troops and civilians alike as being wasted on him. She came from a highly respected family, and since no breath of scandal was ever attached to her actions, she retained a name for dignity and probity. When Farouk was deposed, the press went to some pains to publicize the fact that she never stood in any danger and that she was given the Summer Palace on the Mena Road as a permanent residence.

10. The P-51 was a World War 2 fighter aircraft known as the Mustang.

11. Western Kentucky.

12. Correspondence, Tuck Boys (Bien Hoa Productions, Fayetteville, Arkansas) to Cleveland, 1 July 1988.

13. See Gordon "Inferno," LC.

14. Western Kentucky.

15. Both located at Western Kentucky (Wilgus Collection).

16. Hamilton Collection, 29 March 1947. A USAF contemporary version is located in Getz (1986a).

17. Underwood Collection, Folio 3: Superstitions.

5

The Hungry Warrior

In all the categories of protest, by far the greatest volume of military songs are devoted to complaining about food and grumbling about the conditions of service and the pay, and having to put up with boring or unpleasant places. In "The Regular Army, Oh!" (Dolph 1929*; Loesser 1942), the hungry warrior details the hardships of life in the U.S. Army of the 1870s before the Spanish-American War.[1] He curses the day he marched away to do "forty miles a day on beans and hay," fighting the Indians in Arizona and walking all the way to Mexico, then concludes:

> There's corns upon our heels, my boys
> And bunions on our toes,
> And lugging a gun in the red hot sun
> Puts freckles under our nose;
> England has their Grenadiers
> And France has their Zuzus,
> But the U.S.A. never changes they say,
> Just continues to wear the blues.
> When you're out on parade, boys
> You must have your musket bright
> Or they'll slap you in the guardhouse
> To pass away the night;
> And if you want a furlough
> To the Colonel you do go,
> And he says, "Go to bed,

And wait until you're dead!"
In the regular Army, oh!

Jack Carrol, a field artillery supply corporal in the AEF in France during World War 1, grumbled about the mud,[2] which is one of the concerns of every soldier who has ever endured a winter campaign in Europe.

You sleep in the mud and drink it, that's true;
There's mud in the bacon, the rice and the stew,
When you open an egg, there's mud in it, too!
Sunny France! Etc.

Training camps are another target for indignation, probably because of the severity of the discipline and the shock of comparison between barracks austerity and tantalizing civilian pleasures and comforts. Camp Chaffee was particularly memorable to U.S. troops in World War 2.

In the northern corner of Arkansas
Camp Chaffee is the spot
We are doomed to spend our time
In the land that God forgot.

Down with the snakes and lizards,
Down where a man gets blue,
Right in the midst of nowhere
And a thousand miles from you.

We're soldiers of the 5th Armored,
Earning so little pay,
Guarding people with millions
For two-and-a-half a day.

Living with our memories,
Waiting to see our gals,
Hoping that while we've been gone
They haven't married our pals.

Nobody knows we are living,
Nobody gives a damn;
At home we're all forgotten,
We belong to Uncle Sam.

The time we spend in the army,
The time of our lives we have missed;
Boys, don't let the draft board get you,
And for God's sake don't enlist.

When we die and go to Heaven
To St. Peter we will tell,

We are soldiers of Camp Chaffee
And we've spent our time in HELL![3]

In World War 2, Sampson, a U.S. naval training station at Geneva, New York, also aroused bitter memories in a song that was sung to the tune of "Let's Remember Pearl Harbor."

Let's remember dear Sampson
As a concentration camp,
Let's remember dear Sampson
Where they fed us like tramps.

We will always remember
How we fought for a seven-day pass;
Let's remember dear Sampson,
You can shove it up your ass![4]

Other lyrics current in the U.S. services in World War 2 were scornful of "Puerto Rico, Gem of the Tropics"[5] where "your skin is burned to parchment in the scorching noonday sun/ And you wake up in the morning with a screaming case of runs"; of "Okinawa"[6] (to the tune of "Oklahoma") where we sit "and look across the isles and see some grass,/ but no ass for a distance of six thousand miles"; and of "Somewhere in New Guinea"[7] (to the tune of "Old Man River") where the sun "is like a curse/ and each long day is followed by another slightly worse."

The U.S. Navy lower decks were scathing about Norfolk, a major naval base where God gathered "the wreckage and the tilling, the scum, the sewers and the junk/ And built on the shore of the Chesapeake, the great international dump."[8] In "My Hitch in Hell," the sailor complains that he has "swabbed a thousand bulkheads, chipped a million miles of paint" and that "a cleaner place this side of hell I'll swear there simply ain't." "The Destroyer Song" describes how you "roll and toss and pound and pitch and groan...it's a helluva life on a destroyer" (Niles 1927; Palmer* 1944; Posselt 1943).

U.S. sailors on the China Station sang derisively about the submarine service to the tune of "A Shanty in Old Shanty Town" (Western Kentucky, Wilgus Collection). (A pig-boat is a slang term for a submarine, and "the River" is a reference to the Yangtze Patrol.)

It's only a pig-boat in old Subic Bay,
Its decks are all rusty,
They're rotting away;
It's a broken-down ship
With a broken-down crew,
The Skipper is horse shit,
The Exec's that way too—

I put in for the River
But it didn't go through,
The Skipper said: "Son,
It's the pig-boats for you."
I'll be singing the blues
For the rest of my cruise,
On a pig-boat in old Subic Bay.

Australians fighting in Tobruk on the North African front in World War 2 resorted to a traditional doggerel-verse form of grousing that could be adapted to suit any location and almost any subject. Versions are reproduced in de Witt 1970; Page 1973; Palmer 1944; and Ward-Jackson 1967.

This bloody town's a bloody cuss,
No bloody trams, no bloody bus,
Nobody cares for bloody us!
So bloody! Bloody! Bloody! Etc.

"Never Go to Mersa" (Page 1976) complains about life at Mersa Matruh in the Western Desert during World War 2 where "we eat the flies, we eat the shit, we eat the burning sand . . . but we'll sing our blues away."

New Zealand troops in the same location revived a ballad of Australian origins that depicted Egypt as a land of blazing heat, sweaty socks, sin, sand, pox, harlots, thieves, stink, dirt, sneaking dogs, flies, aching feet, choking dust and Gyppo guts (slang for the stomach disorders to which troops in the desert campaigns of World War 1 and World War 2 were prone).

Similar sentiments were also the burden of an anonymous recitation (from the Cleveland Collection) entitled " 'Ere We Pass." It summarizes the contempt and disgust with which British and Commonwealth troops reacted to contact with wartime Egypt. Shite hawk is slang for the Indian whistling kite, a large scavenging bird common in Egypt. An akker is a slang term for 1 piastre. The bints in the Berkha were prostitutes in the brothel district of Cairo during World Wars 1 and 2. Farouk was the former king of Egypt. Buckshee is slang for free, an adjective derived from Arabic *baaksheesh*, meaning something given for nothing.

If shite hawks were turkeys at an akker apiece
And the sands of the desert were grass,
And the bints in the Berkha were Hollywood stars,
You could stick the whole lot up your arse.

If the streets of old Cairo were covered in gold
And the Wogs there were really high class,

And Farouk gave us each the Star of the Nile,
You could stick the whole lot up your arse.

if taxis and buses were free for The troops
And the trams and the troop trains were fast
And supplied buckshee beer every kilo or so,
You could still stick the lot up your arse.

Now we're leaving old Egypt and bound for our home,
So we'd like to remark 'ere we pass,
If you've room for the Sphinx and the Pyramids too,
Stick the whole bloody lot up your arse.

The "Song of the Afrika Korps" (Hamish Henderson c.1945) is an account of the ordeals of the Fifth Light Motorized Division, the first German formation to arrive in North Africa in 1941. The soldiers got only two litres of water a day and subsisted on dry bread, bad coffee, macaroni and stewed fruit with wine. Their close-cropped heads resembled "bare arses with wings" as they swept through the desert, catching scorpions and snakes and hoping to get some rest in the rear.

Flies, fleas, bugs and insects are a common source of complaint in all armies. Dolph (1929) cites two American Civil War songs about lice-hunting for the creatures that "were always trying to chew armies up." A World War 1 parody of the hymn "Holy, Holy, Holy"[9] is a bitter complaint about exposure to rain and being "lousy in the morning and lousy in the night." A contributor to *Stars and Stripes*[10] thought lice (known as "cooties") were the greatest problem of World War 1 in his verse entitled "A Cootiful Dream" (also reproduced in York 1931).

I dream that somewhere there's water,
Just gobs and gobs in a tub
That steams like geysers in action
And towels, yes Turkish, to rub
My crusted frame to a pinkness
And ivory that's practically pure,
And I fall to hunting the cooties
And pray for my dream to endure. Etc.

Flies inflicted endless torment in the desert campaigns of World War 2. A diarist cited in one of the 2NZEF war histories (Ross 1959:182) complains about billions of corpse-fed flies sending the troops insane. "As I lie here writing this, there are hundreds walking all over me, on my mouth, in my nose, ears, everywhere. . . . Had a cup of tea in the morning and put it down for a second—eight flies in the cup straight away. . . . Had Geoff's complaint today—vomiting and diarrhoea." Such problems were one of the causes of a serious decline in morale in 1942.

A poem published in *NZEF Times*[11] entitled "Desert Troubles" noted that

> We're sick of being pestered
> And almost digested
> By flies.
> The whole blinking army
> is being driven barmy
> By flies. Etc.

In the course of the twentieth century, technology has brought great changes to the control of pests and the mobility of armies, but food continues to be a universal preoccupation of all troops and a primary concern of military occupational lore. According to Palmer (1977:81), the phrase "the hungry army" was almost proverbial in the nineteenth century. He cites a song by this title which satirizes the brutal and deprived conditions of service in the British Army with "General Howl and Scoff" at its head. Farwell (1981: 88) says that the food of the ordinary soldier was miserable. Boiled meat was called "Harriet Lane," this being the name of a woman hacked to pieces by a notorious murderer.

Nor were the commissary arrangements for the American soldier much better. Washington's Revolutionary Army at Valley Forge nearly starved on a diet of "fire cakes" made by spreading a paste of flour and water on a flat stone and up-ending it beside a fire until it was sufficiently charred on the outside. Complaints about being fed on beans, salt meat and hardtack are frequent in the songs of the Union Army in the U.S. Civil War. Commager (1973:297) describes their staple diet as coffee and hardtack—a biscuit also known as hard bread, made of flour and water that was old, wormy and mummified. A surfeit of beans and salt pork required an antiscorbutic, so the government issued dessicated vegetables in sheets like hops "as a substitute for food" (Commager 1973:280).

According to Billings (1888:111–12), a Union soldier was entitled each day to 12 oz of pork or bacon, or 1 lb 4 oz of salt or fresh beef. In addition, he was supposed to receive 1 lb 6 oz of soft bread or flour, but if that was not forthcoming, he was theoretically entitled to either 1 lb of hard bread (hardtack) or 1 lb 4 oz of corn meal. Supposedly, with every hundred of these rations, there should have been distributed one peck of peas or beans, 10 lb of rice or hominy, 10 lb of green coffee (or 8 lb of roasted or ground) or 1 lb 8 oz of tea; 15 lb of sugar; 1 lb 4 oz of candies; 4 lb of soap; two quarts of salt; four quarts of vinegar; 4 oz of pepper; half a bushel of potatoes (when practicable) and one quart of molasses.

This, however, was the camp ration scale. The marching ration was more spartan, consisting of 1 lb of hard bread, 3/4 lb of salt pork or 1 1/4 lb of fresh meat; plus sugar, coffee and salt. Fresh meat was either fried in a lightweight pan or brazed on the end of a stick by the troops. Salt pork (the principal meat ration) was either broiled and eaten with hardtack, made into soup, stewed with baked beans or simply chewed raw between two pieces of hardtack while on the march. Billings (1888:135) describes much of it as musty, rancid, flabby and stringy "sowbelly."

Beans were sometimes baked in ovens of stones made by the cooks or in mess kettles dug into the ground over layers of hot coals. Toward the end of the war, sutlers (who were civilian traders allowed to sell food and other supplies to the troops able to afford them) offered self-rising flour that could be made into fritters or pancakes. All this was rich fare compared to what was available to the Confederate Army, which was far less well supplied. When it was not actually starving, it expressed its disgust in the song about "Eating Goober Peas" (Dolph* 1929), a variety of peanut.

Biscuits and corned beef were the staple diet of British and American troops in World War 1. The Argentinian variety, consumed by the shipload by the AEF, aroused the scorn of *Stars and Stripes* contributors to its Army Poets feature. "I Love Corned Beef" was the ironic title of one typical piece of doggerel.

I love corned beef, I never knew
How good the stuff could taste in stew!
I love it wet, I love it dry,
I love it baked and called meat pie;
I love it camouflaged in hash,
A hundred bucks I'd give in cash
To have a barrel of such chow
Standing here before me now! Etc.[12]

But in World War 1, meat in any form was a luxury to German troops. John Ellis (1976) describes how "Hindenburg Fat" was made of mashed turnip served as a kind of paste with bread made from dried, ground turnips and sawdust. The winter of 1916–17 was known as "the turnip winter." Stew was sometimes made of horsemeat with nettles for vegetables. These were called "barbed wire entanglements." British Army frontline rations were often a diet of hard biscuits that were difficult to chew, tinned bully beef and a variety of stew called Machonochies Meat and Vegetable Ration. Jam was usually plum and apple.

Ernst Junger (1929) complains about being fed on turnips for a whole week and considers the shortage of rations in the German Army during World War 1 to have been one of its most serious problems. In the frontline there was thin soup at mid-day, one-third of a loaf of bread and some mouldy jam. This was augmented by swedes (a colloquial term for rutabaga), barley and dried vegetables with the occasional issue of beans and dumplings. A French officer describing his treatment in German prisoner of war camps[13] said the weekly meat ration was only 3 ounces of raw meat, including bone. The rest of the time, they got swedes and turnip leaves boiled and baptized as spinach. However, the prisoners were able to receive parcels from home that contained tins of meat. The German soldiers guarding them collected the empty tins from the garbage in order to scrape what little grease was left. They would also grab any pieces of green, mouldy bread that arrived spoiled in the parcels. By 1918 German civilians were literally starving. *Stars and Stripes* published a satire on the country's food-rationing difficulties in the form of a wartime meal recipe entitled "The Groaning Board in Germany."

Dip the meat card in the egg card and bake it in the butter card to a nice brown on both sides. The vegetable card is to be steamed with the flour card until partly tender and then cooked with the potato card until done. . . . [14]

The item continues with similar instructions for dessert and then concludes with an instruction to "be sure to remember that the kitchen fire is to be made with a coal card and your hands washed with a soap card and dried on a clothing card."

Rank-and-file protests of life in the World War 1 trenches survived within the German Army into World War 2 in the song "The Captain's Dog." The troops are starving on their turnip diet, which is giving them diarrhoea. But their captain's dog is well fed, the sergeant-major has a warm bed in a dugout and the only people who can get leave are the peasant farmers who are needed to harvest the crops. The following is a translation by Mick Shepherd of a version he collected from Wehrmacht prisoners in North Italy in 1944.

Our Captain had a fat dog;
And turnip jam keeps our arses busy,
And the cold makes your ribs burst
And the troops grow happily fat from lice.

And leave is for the peasant farmers only,
And the troops stay in trenches for a year
And Woodenhead keeps his bedstead warm,
And when well-fried, he sounds roll call.

And the dwindling troops have done their duty,
And in the morning they'll be in the casualty list,

And the war profiteers grow maggot-fat,
And the skeleton of the army rattles on the barbed wire![15]

Such grim chronicles apart, military discussion about food tends to overlook the terrible realities of wartime survival faced by civilian populations for whom food can sometimes be the most important cultural export of an invading or occupying army. One of the present writer's most vivid recollections of the Italian campaign in World War 2 concerns an incident at Forli in 1944 where the battalion was billeted for a time after the town had been captured from the Germans. The writer's company was occupying what had once been a block of apartments that now resembled some abandoned and pillaged ruin in Harlem or the Bronx. It was winter and snow was falling. The company cooks had brought a hot meal around in a truck and were ladling it out as the troops emerged from the building, received their ration and scurried back inside to the luxury of a fire made from broken furniture.

When the writer's turn came, he presented a mug and two crockery plates taken from an abandoned *casa* and received a dollop of stew in one and a generous ladle of rice custard in the other. As he ran back across the street, he slipped, and the contents of both plates splattered on the ice-covered pavement. Immediately a swarm of hungry children who had been intently watching were scrambling at the sticky mess, scraping it up, snow, dirt from the road and all, while one child who had been a little behind the others, knelt face down, licking the last traces from the frozen surface.

During the awful winters of 1944 and 1945, many of the starving populace of North Italy begged for subsistence, turned to prostitution, traded on the black market and sold off whatever possessions they might have managed to retain for the cash to buy food and clothing at vastly inflated prices. A considerable proportion of the rations provided for the Eighth and Fifth armies in Italy was sustaining civilian refugees in the towns. Some of it was being sold on the black market, other parts were exchanged for services and favors and still others given away. Many soldiers made friends with Italian families and gave them food in return for hospitality. When a soldier went visiting, it was the polite thing to take along a pound of sugar, some tea or coffee, a bar of soap, some tinned meat, or the greatest of luxuries, some candy or chocolate.

Most company chow lines were attended by a queue of women and children carrying containers which they were allowed to fill with anything left over. Some units unofficially adopted small boys who had lost their parents and fed and clothed them in return for work around the cookhouse or the quarters. This was rather like the efforts of the AEF in World War 1 to do something about the plight of orphaned French

Traditionally, Western armies have depended on a commissariat supplying bulk food for preparation in cookhouses and subsequent distribution. *Above:* A camp cookhouse in U.S. Civil War. *(National Archives). Below:* Soldiers peeling potatoes in Camp Mills, Mineola, Louisiana, during World War 1. *(National Archives)*

A soldier's standard of living revolves largely around the arrangements for feeding him. These vary from glamorous attention to primitive squalor. Here members of a touring USO variety show serve chow to soldiers of the U.S. 2nd Infantry Division in Korea, 1951. *(National Archives)*

Jokes about cooking and eating were a prominent feature in the *Stars and Stripes* newspaper in World War 1. *(Reproduced from the issue of 5 April 1918)*

Food is an important medium of cultural exchange. These cooks in a New Zealand infantry company are fraternizing with Italian women in a village in North Italy, 1945. *(War History Collection, Alexander Turnbull Library, Wellington, New Zealand)*

A U.S. soldier is greeted with a plate of spaghetti upon entering Messina in the Invasion of Sicily in World War 2. *(National Archives)*

American soldiers
eating pies on their
return from France
in 1919. *(National
Archives)*

Severo N. Rievera,
a trooper in the 1st
Cavalry Division,
eating a coconut
during a break in
search operations in
Bin Dinh Province,
South Vietnam,
June 1967. *(U.S.
Army)*

New Zealand soldiers cooking over a Primus stove in an empty petrol tin in Egypt, 1941
(War History Collection, Alexander Turnbull Library, Wellington, New Zealand)

69th Engineers Battalion troops eating C rations in Vietnam, September 1970. *(U.S. Army)*

25th Infantry Division troops receiving a hot meal in the field while on an operation in Long Thanh Province, South Vietnam, March 1970. *(U.S. Army)*

children. The *Stars and Stripes* ran a scheme by which AEF units, or individual soldiers, could "adopt" a child by paying for its proper housing and nourishment. By the end of 1918, a War Orphans' Continuation Fund had been established to finance the future care and education of some of these children.

The happy Allied warrior in the culinary deserts of World War 1 France, at least around the base camps and rear positions, could sometimes augment his diet by purchasing food from French civilians or by taking advantage of the canteens operated by welfare organizations. These would be anything from a tent, a shed, an old barracks, a disused factory, or a temporary shack made from scraps lying about the rear of the battlefield. The *Stars and Stripes* had particular praise for the Salvation Army. Along with a photograph of one of its women workers in a steel helmet and respirator while rolling dough in a dugout near the front, it ran a few lines of verse in honor of the pleasures of pie.

"Home is where the heart is,"
Thus the poet sang;
But "Home is where the pie is"
For the Doughboy gang.
Crullers in the craters,
Pastry in *abris*,
The Salvation Army lass
Sure knows how to please.[16]

Much metaphoric ingenuity has been devoted to the language of wartime food and eating. In World War 1, stew was known as "slum" by the U.S. Army. This was presumably an attenuation of "slumgullion." Condensed milk was "armoured cow," butter was "axle grease," mess sergeants were "belly robbers," corned beef hash was "canned Willie," sausages were "repeaters," an army cook was a "slum burner" and a rolling kitchen was a "slum cannon" (in the Germany Army it was a "goulash cannon"). French canned meat supplied to the AEF was called "monkey meat," and the *Stars and Stripes* reported that the whole ration question from the soldier's point of view had settled down to finding ways of avoiding making a meal of it.[17]

On Gallipoli in World War 1, Australians described apricot jam as "Deakin's diarrhoea." (Sir Alfred Deakin was leader of the Australian Liberal party.) New Zealand troops in the Pacific theater in World War 2 referred disparagingly to canned meat and vegetable stew as "dog's vomit" and Vienna-style U.S. sausages as "horse cock." Australian tinned mutton, a gruesome commodity issued as rations to some unfortunate U.S. troops in the Pacific, was called "sheep shagnasty" by its ungrateful consumers. Chipped beef on toast was known throughout the U.S. forces as "shit on a shingle."

A verse of "Madamoiselle from Armentieres" collected in 1947 goes:

> If they feed us shit on a shingle again,
> Parlez-vous?
> If they feed us shit on a shingle again,
> Parlez-vous?
> If they feed us shit on a shingle again,
> How in the hell will we ever win?
> Hinky, dinky, parlez-vous?[18]

In U.S. Army mess hall slang during World War 2, a "chow hound" was a big eater, "G Men" were the garbage detail, "buzzard" was turkey, "moo" was cream, "squeak" was pork, "army chicken" was beans and frankfurters, "asshole putty" was cheese and "machine oil" was syrup. "Army strawberries" were prunes, "bags of mystery" were sausages, a "bean gun" was a mobile kitchen, "bubble dancing" was washing dishes, "dog food" or "kennel rations" was corned beef hash, a "hand grenade" was a hamburger, a "hash burner" was a cook and a "tyre patch" was a pancake. In Marine Corps slang, coffee was "jamok," salt was "sea dust," eggs were "hen fruit" and tapioca pudding was "frogs' eyes" or "frogs' balls."

In the Western desert campaigns of World War 2, German Afrika Korps rations were monotonous and limited. They included meat in Italian government cans stamped "A.M." The German soldiers called them *Alter Mann* (old man) or *Amer Mussolini* (poor old Mussolini). The Italians described them as *Asino Morte* (dead donkey).

Although U.S. troops in the song "Chow Down" made jokes about mess hall coffee being good for cuts and bruises and tasting like iodine, with doughnuts that rolled off the table "and killed a friend of mine," in fact motorized transport and improvements in food technology during World War 2 made it possible for vast numbers of troops to be fed more nutritiously than before. Whatever its actual qualities, food also became more portable.

U.S. Army C rations consisted of a tin of instant coffee, some hard candy, four biscuits and a small can either of meat hash, meat and beans, or meat and vegetable stew. This was supposed to provide a meal for one person under combat conditions, but a New Zealand soldier used to large quantities of bread, vegetables and meat could devour six of these rations at a sitting and still complain about being hungry. This was in gastronomic contrast to Japanese infantry who were sustained in combat situations by what was probably the leanest of all diets consisting of about 1 kilogram of rice per day, sometimes delivered in the form of puffed rice pressed into blocks. These could be augmented by poultry, fruit, vegetables and fish that the soldiery had to forage for themselves on the way to an objective.

C rations were issued to troops in the bush in Vietnam. They came in cartons, each containing twelve different meals along with extras like instant coffee, sweets, cigarettes and toilet paper. The cardboard could be used as a mattress, as fuel for fires or as patching for hooches. K rations, in cardboard packages, were designed as a lightweight food supply for men on the move. Dickson (1978:54) mentions that the malt-dextrose tablets and the synthetic lemon powder that were included in them were universally disliked. One mess sergeant used lemon drink as a floor cleaner!

Refrigerated vans and helicopters were used in Vietnam to move fresh food out to fire-support bases, and hot meals were delivered in insulated containers. Lightweight, compressed, freeze-dried combat rations were supplied to troops who could not be reached with hot food. These could either be eaten dry or with the addition of water. In the 1980s the U.S. Army was using 8 ounce packs of ground beef with vegetables that could be reconstituted and heated for individual consumption. Subsequent research and development has concentrated on the irradiation of food in order to destroy bacteria and allow it to be kept for longer periods.

Meanwhile, the U.S. Army's conversion to fast foods represents the ultimate marriage of popular culture and convenience. A traveling fast food stand called the "Wolfmobile" (after its inventor) was tried out in Operation Desert Storm. It supplied a homeland cuisine of burgers, French fries, sodas, hot dogs and grilled cheese sandwiches.

By comparison with all these refinements, the food prepared by the company cooks in New Zealand infantry outfits during World War 2 seems almost barbaric, if more wholesome. It was mainly a monotonous diet of stew, tinned fish or canned meat served with whatever vegetables might be available. This was eked out with rice, porridge, custard powder and any tinned fruit that might occasionally be issued. The whole was augmented with bread, cheese, jam and tea made in large steel containers called "dixies" with milk and sugar added and usually tasting of the chloride of lime used to purify the water.

The cooks' efforts were limited by what items they could get from the quartermasters' stores, by the technology at their disposal and by the amount of time within which meals had to be prepared. Everything had to be managed with pressurized petrol burners in a highly mobile outfit that was in continual movement. This method of cooking could, within a few hours, produce a meal of sorts for 130 or so men (the average strength of an infantry company), but there were no roasting or grilling facilities and this rather limited what could be managed.

During the summer, and when their clientele were not in the frontline, most company cooks tried to improve their offerings by using regimental funds to purchase extra fruit and vegetables from any civilian sources that might be available. In the static circumstances of the Italian campaign, it was sometimes possible for the cooks to prepare more elaborate meals by using the ovens and kitchens of the civilian premises they occupied. When lines of communication between the front and the rear were secure, meals could be prepared and packed into portable hot boxes that could be taken forward by jeep and then backpacked into frontline positions at night. (Today they would more likely be flown in by helicopter.) Otherwise, in combat situations, the infantry subsisted on a diet of hard biscuits, bread, bully beef, canned meat and vegetable ration, canned pilchards in tomato sauce, tinned bacon, tinned margarine, jam, cheese and tinned sausages made out of soya beans and tasting like sawdust. All this was likely to be augmented by anything the troops could loot, steal or forage for themselves.

Wherever possible, they brewed their own tea on Primus stoves procured with money from patriotic funds, on lightweight gasoline burners captured from the Wehrmacht or on stoves and fires lit in whatever buildings they might be occupying. In most battalions, the custom was for each infantry section to maintain its own private pool of extra tinned rations in a steel artillery ammunition container for use in rest areas and rear positions. The container stored the contents of food parcels mailed from home, along with any extras that could be purchased from canteens, filched from army stores or acquired as loot. The section boxes were carted about in the B echelon transport along with each soldier's personal kitbag, the extra platoon and company weapons, reserve ammunition and all the other impedimenta of a company of heavy infantry. They were used to improve the official scale of meals with feeds of tinned whitebait, oysters and other delicacies from the homeland. These were cooked and consumed at the small-group level in the infantry sections.

This additional catering was not part of the formal organization of the battalion but had been devised by the infantry themselves as a way of making life less miserable and more hospitable. At impromptu festive occasions, the section boxes provided food that could be shared, especially with visitors. They also made it possible to pool the surplus contents of food parcels from home, so that everyone in the group had a share. A singsong or a bull session in the lines would usually conclude with a brew of tea on one of the section stoves and the cooking of some canned provisions from the box. Home was wherever the section box might be, along with the stove and somewhere to lie down. As cultural equipment, the section box was a focus for group relaxation and hospitality that also conveyed a definition of location and a sense of occupancy, no matter how transient, of hostile space. Soldiers tended to congregate around it like gypsies at a hearth in some temporary encampment, or like a tribal hunting group gathered at their cooking fire in the wilderness.

Section boxes as an artifact of material culture also added a modest private dimension to the soldier's life. Their contents were entirely at their owners' personal disposal to consume or distribute as they pleased, while the cooking of occasional unscheduled meals and snacks enabled them to indulge themselves with items that were not standard army fare. So, while the section box gave its owners extra group cohesion by acting as a catalyst for sociability, it also allowed each individual soldier some personal freedom to eat whatever he pleased when it suited him.

The section box plus the bed or blanket roll were the chief comforts of the soldier's uncertain existence. Beds that would actually lift a sleeper off the ground were luxuries in World War 2. Frontline infantry lived, slept and ate in whatever holes, trenches, dugouts or corners of buildings they were fighting from. In rear areas during the Italian summer, there were bivouacs in the fields among the grapevines, but in winter the troops sought shelter indoors. They slept in barns and farmhouses, on the ground or on stone floors with their blankets spread over a gas cape. This was a thin, waterproof, outer garment like a poncho that was issued as personal protection against the possible use of skin-irritant poison gases. They made convenient raincoats and covers for weapons.

In one small town where the present writer's platoon was billeted, a soldier thought himself lucky to purloin a wooden gate that he used to raise himself a few inches from the floor. In the fields alongside a fighter strip at Riccione on the Adriatic coast, others made beds that were supported on two ammunition boxes out of sections of perforated metal strip that they unhooked from the end of the runway when nobody was looking. Another soldier writing home[19] announced with delight that his outfit had moved into a former boarding school and acquired beds and mattresses. In spite of holes in the roof and lack of doors and windows, they were "pretty comfortable." This was high-class accommodation roughly equivalent in peacetime to some homeless itinerant being put up at the Hilton.

Drivers of vehicles were always better off. Most of them had mattresses fitted into the trucks they drove, and they usually had a store of personal goodies secreted somewhere about their vehicles along with a Benghazi burner. This cylindrical, kettlelike device was made of sheet metal and heated a small, built-in cannister of water by means of a petrol fire lit in a tray of sand at its base. It was the standard method for boiling water for tea throughout the Division and was probably responsible for much of its huge fuel consumption.

For all their care with the details of personal survival and their ingenuity in improvising beds and al fresco meals, New Zealand soldiers

were receptive consumers of tales like the erroneous belief that chemicals
were put in the soldiers' food to reduce the frequency of sexual arousal.
To the tune of the hymn "There Is a Happy Land," they sang this
mournful complaint (from the Cleveland Collection).

> I know an army camp
> Not far away,
> Where we get bread and cheese
> Three times a day;
> Ham and eggs we never see,
> They put killcock in all the tea,
> So we are gradually
> Fading away.

Rich and Jacobs (1973) attribute the general military fascination with
saltpetre and other antiaphrodisiacs to the soldier's need for adjustment
to sexual tensions brought about by the stress of military life. They
suggest that much of the military folklore dealing with food has similar
origins. The hungry warrior's obsession with food and his complaints
about its quality are therefore an expression of his displaced anxieties.
No matter how much effort a well-intentioned command might make
to improve the living standards of its troops, grumbling about food will
continue as long as its underlying psychological causes remain.

Even though the commander of the N.Z. Division in World War 2
(Major General Bernard C. Freyberg) was exceptionally attentive to the
food and general welfare of the ordinary soldier, a satire entitled "General
Freyberg's Stew" was nevertheless sung at concerts around the divisional
area in the Middle East. In this song (see Cleveland 1991:89),
the cooks are discovered "chanting out in rhythm, that's the stuff to give
'em" as they concoct a mixture of camel, donkey, shite hawk, half a bottle
of Stella,[20] a motor tyre, some beans, half a ton of buffalo dung, a
hundredweight of sand and two coconuts for the hungry warrior's unappreciative
sustenance.

The subsistence behavior of the military is socially important. On the
one hand, solo cooking and unofficial meals are an assertion of individuality,
a breakaway from the imposed uniformity of the issue rations,
an exercise in alternative, personal tastes and a lapse in the tyranny of
military order. On the other hand, food sharing and especially communal
eating, is a communicative act that adds to social cohesion.

In static situations in barracks, posts and fixed bases, this subsistence
behavior operates at several levels. The segregation of officers and senior
NCOs in clubs and messes strengthens their identity as separate castes,
while the bulk feeding of standardized meals to other ranks in canteens,
mess halls and chowlines brings the economies of scale to bear on com-

missariat arrangements and imparts a convenient unity to company, regimental or whatever organizational configuration might be present.

Thus, fighter pilots, whose relationship to their aircraft is tightly integrative and routinized, set great store by the social interactions and symbolism of eating and drinking together, perhaps the more so because their flying duties are so technology-dependent and essentially lonely. Tuso (1990:16–18) gives an account of the importance of the regular, ritual gatherings of his squadron in Vietnam in a formal atmosphere of feasting, fellowship and entertainment in the officers' club. This was the center of their social life where they ate all their meals "in an all-male, war-oriented, closed social group."

In the more primitive field locations of the infantry, preparing food and eating it are central to the life of the primary combat groups. Gathering round a fire, a small stove or some other means of heating rations is a social event that provides opportunities for conversation among participants and offers the reassurance of at least a token fraternity of sharing in a social context that is not completely dictated by the machinery of war and is to some extent under the individual soldier's direct control. This has some parallels with the practice described by McCarl (1985) whereby firemen cooked their own meals in the fire house, shared in the work of preparation and ate together. It was an important social event that underscored the closeness of the group.

Contradictory forces are at work in the life of the hungry warrior. The increasing feminization of the armed services and the greater presence of women in the ranks may lead to more sensitivity about catering and the social arrangements for eating. However, advances in food technology may now be reducing the informal opportunities for socialization in the field because of the use of combat ration packs that do not require communal preparation and can be carried and consumed individually without reliance on fires, stoves or other methods of heating. In this situation calculated obsolescence could have important advantages.

The section boxes carried about for the use of the infantry platoons of the N.Z. Division in World War 2 used up transport space and were a bulky nuisance, but they did more for morale than any other single factor in the short lives of their beneficiaries. The crude cooking practices at Valley Forge and the tins of C rations heated up in foxholes in World War 2 and Korea, for all the grumbling aroused by their monotonous contents, were the means for humble enactments of small-scale solidarity. Today's improvements in cuisine are aimed at giving the individual soldier more portable, more easily prepared, precooked meals that offer greater personal choice and quality of menu. But are these improvements at the expense of the social linkages without which soldiers cannot fight effectively? Today's troops may be better fed, but will they, in consequence, become lesser warriors?

NOTES

1. Gordon Collection, LC. Gordon collected many variants of this song which appears to have been well known in the 1920s. One informant told him that the last time he heard it was in 1917 in the 1st Cavalry Division at El Paso, Texas, where an effort was made to use it as a marching song. The reference to French "Zuzus" is probably an attempt at Zouaves.

2. *Stars and Stripes*, 7 June 1918, p. 7.

3. Western Kentucky (Wilgus Collection).

4. Hamilton Collection.

5. Indiana. To the tune of "On the Road to Mandalay."

6. Hamilton Collection.

7. Indiana.

8. Indiana. Collected in 1942.

9. See Brophy and Partridge (1965).

10. 15 November 1918, p. 14.

11. 7 September 1942, p. 5.

12. 5 July 1918, p. 4.

13. *Stars and Stripes*, 26 April 1918, p. 2.

14. 19 April 1918, p. 7.

15. A German vernacular version of the World War 1 original is given in Zweig (1961:191). Its performance is forbidden by the staff, but the soldiers burst out with it in fury and despair.

16. 26 April 1918, p. 4.

17. 28 June 1918, p. 2.

18. Hamilton Collection.

19. Cleveland Collection.

20. Stella was an Egyptian wartime beer that tasted strongly of onions.

6

The Mortal Warrior

Death is the ultimate fate that every warrior may be called upon to encounter, but the military's treatment of it is inclined to be evasive. Realistic consideration of the statistical probabilities of becoming a wartime casualty, and how the candidates might fortify themselves psychologically against the disquieting possibility of death or wounding in battle, tends to be omitted from training schedules and obscured by the sentimental fantasies of popular culture. This omission can mask the realities of death both in religious ritual and in secular concepts of duty that expect the warrior to accept the necessity for sacrifice in the nation's service. Concepts of manliness and honor also enjoin the potential casualty to show a cool unconcern in the face of danger and to do his duty when called upon. Only in religious counseling and in some aspects of expressive behavior can the warrior indicate his very real fears or take refuge in superstitious rituals and in the singing of songs that admit his fragile mortality.

Soldiers' songs that deal with death and suffering, and grim jokes about the lethal nature of the battlefield, are a mediation between life and death and a way of psychologically confronting its terrors. Singing and joking about them turns a private nightmare into an item of public debate and reduces its power by bringing it under a degree of social control. To bring death into the gambit of everyday discourse is to familiarize its inevitability. Thus, the frightful casualty rate and the daily horrors of trench warfare in World War 1 seemed to condition the participants to a wry acceptance of fate that is apparent in this lament that was still circulating in the 1920s.

> Born in South Carolina,
> Raised in Tennessee,
> Worked like hell in Georgia,
> Died in Germany.[1]

The miseries of hospitalization were chronicled in grim little satires like the veterans' "Please May I Have a Pension" (Cleveland 1959; Getz 1986a) to the tune of "My Bonnie Lies Over the Ocean."

> For forty long years I've been hounded
> By all sorts of horrible pains,
> I've had every ailment, I reckon
> From rupture to varicose veins.
>
> Neuritis with me is a hobby,
> I've bunions and corns on my feet,
> While I seem to grow lumps there inside me
> Like ruddy great chunks of concrete.
>
> I've spent a small fortune on chemists
> And lain months in hospital beds,
> And the stuff that I've taken to aid me
> Has torn my intestines to shreds. Etc.

Another doleful World War 1 complaint, to the tune of "Broken Doll," catalogued some of the distress of amputation.

> I lost my poor old leg a year ago,
> They told me they were making legs for show;
> I soon learned what pain was,
> I thought I knew;
> My poor old stump is slowly turning
> Red, white and blue;
> The matron said, "You're walking very well,"
> I told her she could take the leg to hell,
> And as I limped away
> My comrades did say,
> I see you've got a Rowley too.[2]

"The Lousy Lance-Corporal," sung to the tune of "Villikins And His Dinah," accepts death as the likely outcome of bravery and protests against injustice. Versions of this ballad were current among Australian and New Zealand soldiers in World War 1 when they fought together in a combined Australia and New Zealand Army Corps (ANZAC) and again in World War 2. A variant of it emerged among Australians in Vietnam. (This is discussed in Chapter 7.) Texts of "The Lousy Lance-Corporal" are reproduced in Cray 1969* and 1992*; Cleveland 1959, 1961*, 1982* and 1991*; Lahey* 1965; McGregor 1972; Page 1973; Tate 1982; Ward 1964; and York 1931. In these texts the Digger (a popular appellation for any Australian or New Zealand soldier) goes on leave in London from "the shambles of France" but is rebuked by an officious NCO on the headquarters' staff for being improperly dressed. He protests angrily about the conduct of the war "where brave men are dying for bastards like you!"

> A Digger just landed and straight away strode
> To Army Headquarters on Horseferry Road,[3]
> To see all the bludgers[4] who work all the graft[5]
> By getting soft jobs on the headquarters staff.
>
> *Chorus:*
>
> Dinky-die! Dinky-die![6]
> By getting soft jobs on the headquarters staff.
>
> Now a lousy[7] Lance-Corporal said, "Pardon me please,
> You've mud on your tunic[8] and blood on your sleeve,
> If you don't wipe it off all the people will laugh"[9]
> Said that lousy Lance-Corporal on headquarters staff.
>
> The Digger just gave him a murderous glance;
> He said, "I've just come from the shambles of France
> Where whizzbangs[10] are flying and comforts are few
> And brave men are dying for bastards like you."
>
> Dinky-die! Dinky-die!
> Where brave men are dying for bastards like you.
>
> We're bombed on the left and we're bombed on the right,
> We're shelled all the day and we're shelled all the night,
> And if something don't happen and that mighty soon
> There'll be nobody left in the fucking platoon!
>
> Dinky-die! Dinky-die!
> There'll be nobody left in the fucking platoon.
>
> Now all of this came to the ears of Lord Gort[11]
> Who gave the whole matter a good deal of thought;
> He awarded the Digger V.C. and two bars
> For giving that corporal a kick up the arse.
>
> Dinky-die! Dinky-die!
> For giving that corporal a kick up the arse!

The Digger, striding with grim purpose to army headquarters to make his protest, voices all the anger of the frontline soldier toward people who are safe in base establishments where they can exert power over those who do the actual fighting. The Lance-Corporal is the repulsive symbol of a murderous military system, and the shambles of France is the result of a monstrous perversion of technology. Ultimate doom is envisaged in the context ("if something don't happen and that mighty soon"), but the shock of this forecast is mediated by the degree to which it is assumed to be a fate that can somehow be endured collectively, in this case by the platoon. So on their behalf, the Digger speaks out in apprehension, "brave men are dying . . . nobody left in the fucking platoon."

Perhaps Lord Gort represents the principle of natural justice administered by an authority which, because of its fairness in this particular case, is acceptable to men who value egalitarian relationships as a natural right. This is an interesting administration of the principle of justice because it seems at first to depart from the attitudes toward authority held by Australian soldiers as inheritors of the tradition of the "noble bushman."[12]

This is a libertarian, collectivist view of life that is accompanied by a defiance of military bureaucracy, police and all other authoritarian aspects of government. It expressed itself in wartime as a strong resentment of the system of "officers."[13] Here, however, by not upholding the petty authority of the Lance-Corporal and by recognizing the heroism of the ordinary frontline soldier, an aristocratic representative of the disliked officer class has performed a judicial act that fully satisfies the most sensitive egalitarian conscience. It also provides the ballad with an emphatic ending. When singing it in World War 2, performers usually made a crescendo out of the word "kick" by shouting it out as loudly as possible.

Such songs mediate between the intolerable oppositions of free life and the destructive perversions and oppressions of military technology. However, they do not directly challenge the supremacy of the military order but serve to promote it by contributing an alternative mechanism of social control whereby the disillusioned and apprehensive warrior can be brought to accept his fate after he has made his protest.

In World War 2, the statistical incidence of death in the Allied armies was much lower than it had been in World War 1 because improvements were made in the medical treatment of battle casualties and because the larger numbers of people in lines of communication and other rear services were less exposed to frontline combat. Nevertheless, up at the sharp end, death continued to be regarded as the likely fate of the combat soldier. This was the assumption in a cycle of songs that cited the World War 2 warrior's last morbid words as he expired in a variety of unpleasant places. Some of these compositions parodied a traditional American cowboy lyric entitled, alternatively, "Bury Me Out on the Prairie" or "I've

Got No Use for the Women" (Tinsley* 1981:184–88). For example, British Eighth Army soldiers in North Africa in World War 2 sang about the death of "a poor British Tommy."

> 'Twas down at a place called Benghazi
> Where most of the fighting was done,
> 'Twas there that a poor British Tommy
> Was shot by an old Eytie gun.
>
> Leaning himself on his shoulder,
> These were the last words he said:
> "Bury me out on the desert,
> My duty to England is done.
>
> And when you get back to old Blighty
> And the fighting is over and done,
> Just think of the lads in Benghazi
> Under the Libyan sun."[14]

This elegy then concludes with a stanza that is closely imitative of the principal theme of "I've Got No Use for the Women" who, in the original, are depicted as the cause of the cowboy's downfall.

> "I don't give a damn for the women,
> They laugh at you when you are gone,
> They were the cause of my sorrow
> Under the Libyan sun."

A variant current in the N.Z. Division in North Africa in 1940–41 enlarges on this theme of female culpability by attributing the soldier's downfall to a combination of the fleshly corruptions of Egypt and the army itself.[15] The song's morbid view of sexual relationships reflects the general fear of venereal diseases, which was a serious health risk before penicillin came into general use as a treatment later in the war.

> Oh I've a sad story to tell you,
> A story you ain't heard before,
> Concerning my sad adventures
> At the time of the second Great War.
>
> One night as I strolled down the Berkha,[16]
> That horrible street of ill fame,
> Got to know all the dirty old harlots,
> Got to know them all by their names.
>
> There was Susan and Tarzan and Lulu,[17]
> They did it this way and that,

They copied the gestures of animals,
Even the dog and the cat.

They lay on their backs and their bellies,
They charged ten akkers[18] a time;
And if you had *felousse* in your pocket[19]
You could get a good place in the line.[20]

Oh now I am fed up with Egypt,
This land of sin, pox and shame,
Where I lost my good reputation
And only the army's to blame.

Oh bury me out on the desert
Where the shite hawks may pick at my bones;[21]
With a bottle of Pilsener beside me,[22]
So I won't be so very alone.

In another version entitled "Bury Me Out in the Jungle" (Page 1973), a soldier in a British regiment falls to a Japanese gun "at a place called Kohima."[23] This was the scene of bitter, close-quarter fighting in Burma during World War 2. During the Korean War, the poor British Tommy was transformed into a Commonwealth soldier who is shot on the banks of the Imjin by a Communist gun (Page 1976).[24] Finally, New Zealand infantry engaged in antiterrorist duties during the Malaysian emergency had a version that used the tune of "The Old Tarpaulin Jacket." The Bren gun was a light machine gun then in use as standard equipment among British and Commonwealth forces, but presumably in this case in wrong hands since C.T. is the military acronym for Communist terrorist.[25] The *ulu* is vernacular usage for the jungle terrain in which this particular war was fought.

I'll sing you a song of Malaya,
That's where the fighting was done,
And that's where a poor Kiwi soldier
Was hit by a C.T. Bren gun.

While raising himself on one shoulder
With blood dripping down from his head,
He looked at the soldiers around him
And these were the last words he said.

On carry me out from the *ulu*,
Out from the Malayan sun,
Oh carry me back to New Zealand,
My fighting for freedom is done.

In this song cycle, the melodrama of death is dramatized in lurid stereotypes that have little correspondence with battlefield actualities perhaps because the concept of death is more bearable this way, and also because of the artistic difficulties of composition confronting the parodist working almost exclusively with models drawn from the popular culture. Yet the Lousy Lance-Corporal's stark, descriptive utterance about being continuously bombed and shelled is much more compelling than anything the poor British Tommy and his successors have to say, suggesting that apprehension and morbidity need not collapse into doggerel absurdity, provided that the necessary expressive talent is brought to bear.

For instance, the songs of Polish soldiers fighting on the Allied side in World War 2 reached an intensity of lyric sensitivity as well as vehemence in their treatment of fate and alienation from the homeland. "Myśmy tutaj szli" ("We Walked Here"), composed at Latrun in the Western Desert (Leo* 1944), describes the diverse origins of the Carpathian Brigade and the situation of the Polish soldier as "a homeless warrior for ever." (See Appendix.) The dreadful fate of so many Polish soldiers in German and Russian prison camps is implicit in "Coś tyza jeden" ("Who Are You?") in Leo* (1944).

> What sort of a man are you my friend?
> Because you are dressed in a funny way.
> "I am a prisoner of war,
> All I have left from my uniform
> Is my collar
> And a coat that has been repaired
> By the wind." Etc. (Author's translation)

These songs also contain passionate assertions of Polish nationalism, which at that time was dedicated to the war against the Nazis and the fight for national autonomy. This struggle was seen as "the soldier's fate and doom" in which death, as a historical necessity, was equated with honor. "Cerwone maki na Monte Cassino" ("The Red Poppies of Cassino"), composed in the field by Feliks Konarski, a Polish soldier involved in the battle for the fortress, describes the attack on the enemy hiding in the ruins like rats and the epic struggle to plant the Polish flag on the summit. The severity of the Polish casualties is symbolized by the redness of the wild poppies which "drank Polish blood instead of dew." (See Appendix.)

There are few examples of such passionate eloquence in the songs of other Allied troops in World War 2. Nor do they deal so directly with the concept of death as the inevitable price of freedom and honor. For most World War 2 soldiers the concept of death was masked by euphemisms like bowled, hit, kaput, skittled, clobbered, had his time, had his chips, kicked the bucket, gone for a skate, gone for the high jump, bought it, bought one, out of the service, got a wooden overcoat, got three bits of phone wire, won't be coming Monday, lost the number of his mess, got planted, playing a harp and out the monk. This last metaphor (derived from the gambling game of two-up) was used by New Zealanders to describe either death or states of insensibility or unconsciousness that were not necessarily brought about by violence (e.g., sleep or drunkenness).

When the writer's company commander in North Italy called everyone together after they had been enjoying a few weeks of inactivity in a rear position and said sternly: "We're going in to see the Angry Man again," everyone knew they had to go back to the frontline where, inevitably, some would be killed or wounded. There was no mention of death, but it was implicit in what was said and in all the procedures set in motion by this laconic announcement. The epithet "Angry Man" in this context meant *Tu*, the god of war in Maori mythology.[26] Perhaps this invocation of the supernatural helped to bring the fear of death into perspective by placing it in the cultural context of warriorlike deeds, courage and fighting qualities exemplified by the god. It also set the more prudent to overhauling personal weapons and composing last letters home, while the more affluent put their finances in order, left valued possessions with friends in the rear and gave away or destroyed any remainder that could not be carried.

Among infantry generally, technique requires that the concept of death be treated with respectful reticence the closer they are to its actualities. For example, metaphors for killed in common use in Vietnam were zapped, dinged, greased, wasted, blown away, bought the ranch and caught his lunch. Thorpe (1967) mentions that among naval aviators there was a taboo on the expression of fear, while euphemisms like "bought the farm" were used for death. This prohibition does not seem to have extended to the general sphere of occupational song that appears to admit a wider, more open treatment of the probabilities of terminal disaster in the lives of aviators generally. They have always been quick to recognize that death is a likely outcome of combat or a familiar consequence of mechanical failure, pilot error or bad luck. "Stand to Your Glasses" (Getz 1981 and 1986b*; Smith* n.d.; Wallrich 1957; Winstock* 1970; and Ward-Jackson 1945) is thought to have originated in the British Army during the Indian Mutiny. It survived through World War 1 and World War 2 in several versions as an airman's defiant and melodramatic gesture toward the possibility of disaster.

> So stand to your glasses, steady,
> This world is made of lies;
> Here's a toast to the dead already
> And hurrah for the next man to die!

We loop in the purple twilight,
We spin in the silvery dawn,
With a trail of black smoke behind us
To show where our comrades have gone. Etc.

"Blood Upon the Risers" (Burke 1989; Getz 1981), sung to the tune of "The Battle Hymn of the Republic," is a lurid account of the consequences to the paratrooper of an error or malfunction of equipment. The risers are the leads that connect the body harness of a parachute to the canopy above. The lyric envisages a grisly mixture of blood, brains and intestines resulting from a failed jump.

The incidence of death among tail gunners in the bomber aircraft of World War 2 was so high that "The Song of the Aerial Gunner"[27] (sung to the tune of "My Bonny Lies Over the Ocean") accepts this fate as a statistical certainty. This is another example of the discrepancy between wartime sentimentality and brutal actuality. Since World War 1, it has been the custom for the family or close relatives of U.S. services personnel absent on active wartime duty to display a small service flag in the window with either a blue or a silver star for each absent warrior. In the event of his or her demise, the star can be replaced with a gold one.

Take down that blue star, mother,
Replace it with one made of gold;
Your son is an aerial gunner,
He'll die when he's 18 years old.

Chorus:

Tough shit, tough shit,
He'll die when he's 18 years old;
Tough shit, tough shit,
He'll die when he's 18 years old.

They promised him a chest full of ribbons,
They gave him a chest full of lead,
They made him an aerial gunner
And now the poor bastard is dead!

Tough shit etc.

A terse Marine Corps variant emerged in the Korean War.[28] A B.A.R. man operated the Browning automatic rifle with which each squad was equipped. An F.M.F. corpsman was a member of the Fleet Marine Force carrying out medical duties. The force was available for amphibious operations and in this case was used to make a landing at Inchon.

Take down that silver star, mother,
Replace it with one made of gold,
Your son was a fine B.A.R. man,
But he died at 19 years old.

Chorus:

Tough shit, tough shit,
Tough shit, you all.

Your son was an F.M.F. corpsman,
He wore a little band of red,
He lies on the sands of Korea
With 69 holes in his head.

Tough shit etc.

On a hillside in old Korea
Where the grass is never green,
There lies some poor bastard,
A United States Marine.

Tough shit etc.

Other variants of this song pour scorn on those who have managed to get safe jobs back home. The Hamilton Collection contains a contemptuous treatment of the college cadets who were selected for the Army Specialized Training Program in World War 2.

Take down your service flag mother,
Your son's in the ASTP;
He'll never get wounded in battle
Extracting the square root of three.

Chorus:

Bring back, bring back,
Oh bring back my slide rule to me, to me;
Bring back, bring back,
Oh bring back my slide rule to me.

Some mothers have sons in the Army,
Others have sons in Navee,
But take down your service flag mother,
Your son's in the ASTP.

Bring back etc.

A Vietnam version draws a sardonic comparison between the survival prospects of a gunner in a helicopter and a college student in the Reserve Officers' Training Corps.

The symbolism of death is widely used in battlefield propaganda. Here the naked body of a beautiful woman represents life and the instinct of self-preservation while the helmet surmounting a skull signifies the possibility of death in this German propaganda leaflet used in World War 2. *(Cleveland Collection)*

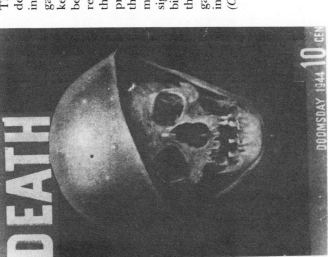

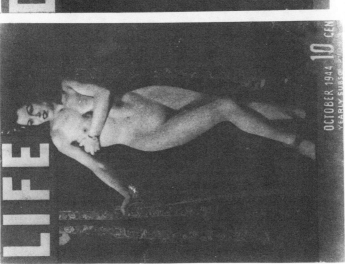

German propaganda used in North Italy in 1945 emphasized the fearful prospects awaiting Allied soldiers in any attempt to cross the Po River against enemy opposition. *(Cleveland Collection)*

Traditionally the helmet placed on a cross, or on an inverted rifle, indicates the location of a battlefield grave, in this case that of three German soldiers near Montoro at Salerno, Italy, September 1943. *(National Archives)*

Jokes about the hazards of battle help to bring fear of death under control. Bruce Bairnsfather, a World War 1 British illustrator, invented a character called "Old Bill," who specialized in a kind of lunatic stoicism. *(Reprinted with the permission of Macmillan Publishing Company from Carry on Sergeant by Bruce Bairnsfather. Copyright 1927 by the Bobbs-Merrill Company, renewed 1954 by Bruce Bairnsfather.)*

After a sharp rise in real estate

Battles wouldn't be half so bad, if only they supplied safety zones where one could get a rest now and then

Religious services are another way of reducing some of the anxieties of combat. A U.S. Army Chaplain conducts a service for troops about to embark on the D-Day assault on Occupied Europe, 1944. *(National Archives)*

Oh take down your service flag mother,
And turn that blue star into gold,
Your boy is a Huey door gunner,
He'll die 'fore he's 20 years old.

Some mothers have sons in the Army,
Some mothers have sons out at sea,
But take down that service flag mother,
Your boy's just in ROTC.[29]

Another song from the Vietnam War ("The Body Bag Song," to the tune of "The Camptown Races")[30] manufactures macabre comedy out of violent death and dismemberment. An RPG is a rocket-propelled grenade.

Hit him in the chest with an RPG,
Do da, do da!
Hit him in the chest with an RPG,
Oh! Do da day!

He ain't got but an arm and a leg,
Do da, do da!
He ain't got but an arm and a leg,
Oh! Do da day!

Send him home in a body bag,
Do da, do da!
Send him home in a body bag,
Oh! Do da day!

Oh, gwine to fight all night,
Gwine to fight all day,
Gwine to send him home in a body bag
All the do da day!

The epistolary form is convenient for ballad composers struggling to express their experiences. They seem to feel an intuitive need to bear witness in a very literal way to the mistakes, terrors and deaths they have encountered and to cite real people and actual events as a kind of shield against chaos and a reassurance that it has not happened to them. "Hullo Father, Dearest Mom"[31] (Davis* 1987) is an example of this documentary style in which the singer explains to his parents that he is in Vietnam, giving them a doleful account of how various acquaintances have been injured or killed.

"Dear Mom" (Durham* 1971; In Country* 1991) is an account of the random death of an infantry soldier in which his mother is informed that her son died heroically "defending the land we all love best."

Some of the ballads of Dick Jonas, a Vietnam War fighter pilot and a prolific composer and singer (1985*; 1987a*; 1987b*), commemorate the violent demise of contemporaries. In one case, "the fireball down there on the hillside" marks the death of a wingman; in another, a pilot is said to have died a hero's death "the way we all would go." Another song tells of an F-5E pilot who deliberately dives his aircraft into the ground, screaming, "That's how a fighter pilot should die!" The death wish implicit in such exploits and sentiments marks the ultimate stage in the morbid integration of man and machine.

Graveyard humor and black comedy embrace the morally objectionable, the monstrous or the demoralizing to the point where they become a paradoxical inversion of all the sentiments normally associated with anxiety, suffering and death. For instance, much of the humor of the television series "M.A.S.H." depends on a flow of wisecracks and outrageous pranks as the medical team processes a never-ending stream of battle casualties. As Captain ("Hawkeye") Pierce puts it: "Joking is the only way of opening my mouth without screaming."[32]

Similarly, jokes about wounding and mortality are the frontline soldier's mordant protection against demoralization, although in some cases they may also function as an indulgence in the emotions of fear and dread for the sake of morbid excitement or amusement. So "The Hearse Song" to the tune of "The Funeral March" (Dolph* 1929; Getz 1981; Loesser 1942; Posselt 1943; and Sandburg* 1927) extracts dour comedy from the funeral ceremony and from contemplation of the processes of bodily decomposition as "the worms crawl in, and the worms crawl out" after you are taken away in "that big, black hack." "When the Guns Are Calling Yonder"[33] (to the tune of "When the Roll Is Called Up Yonder") is a gruesome exploration of the terrible effects of artillery bombardments in World War 1.

> You'll be lying in the rain
> With the shrapnel in your brain
> And you'll never see your sweetheart any more,
> And there'll be no more to tell
> If you're near a bursting shell
> And you'll never see your sweetheart any more.
>
> *Chorus:*
> When the guns are rolling yonder,
> When the guns are rolling yonder,
> When the guns are rolling yonder,
> (Spoken) A BATTERY FALL IN!
> When the guns are rolling yonder we'll be there.
>
> You'll be hanging out your tongue
> When the gas gets in your lung,
> And you'll never see your sweetheart any more;

You'll be splashed with mud and mire
And get washed with liquid fire
And you'll never see your sweetheart any more.

There'll be a red gap in your jacket
When the Pirate gets his bracket,[34]
And you'll never see your sweetheart any more;
You'll miss your next inspection
When the Hun gets his deflection
And you'll never see your sweetheart any more.

The Kaiser and the kite
Have a healthy appetite,
And you'll never see your sweetheart any more;
The jackal and the crow
Say that life was ever so,
And you'll never see your sweetheart any more.

With the advent of aerial warfare and the development of the techniques of bombing and rocketry, no one can be completely safe anywhere near a modern battlefield—the more so as some weapons are indiscriminate in their effects against civil and military targets alike. This new reality inspired U.S. aviators in Korea to modify a World War 1 song about the sinking of "The Great Ship Titanic" (Wallrich 1957) to suit situations where people in a church were hit by rockets or peasants in the fields were destroyed with napalm. Getz (1981) reproduces Korean as well as Vietnam versions of this song, along with a choruslike lament that repeats the line, "It was sad when my napalm went down."

Another song that Getz (1981) considers has Korean War origins describes napalm as "pretty to watch," while yet another entitled "Chocolate-Covered Napalm" in Getz (1981) and Tuso (1990) is a protest, composed like an advertising jingle, against one of the most disturbing aspects of the Vietnam War in which the deadly substance falls from the sky and "makes the people fry!"

The possibility that his aircraft was quite likely to become his coffin troubled the pilot of World War 1 and has continued to haunt aviators ever since. "The Bomber's Lament" (Getz 1981) complains that the De Havilland DH-4 biplane was "a damned flying hearse." It was used by AEF flyers in World War 1 and was notorious for being nose-heavy, sluggish at high altitudes, cranky on the controls and impossible to see from except to the sides and rear. It was known as the "Flaming Four" because its large, exposed fuel tank tended to catch fire during combat. Another song about its shortcomings entitled "The D.H." is a parody of a World War 1 popular lyric, "N' Everything" by Budde Silvia, Gus Kahn and Al Jolson. The D.H. had "a pair of wings tied with strings," and when you did a tailspin, the tail flew free, "and everything." This song is an example of jesting about the probabilities of disaster, as well as an illustration of the crucial importance of technique to the aviator whose life literally depends on knowledge about equipment and his ability to operate it as skillfully as possible to whatever the prevailing standard of performance might be.

The subsequent development of bombing as a method for destroying an enemy's industrial, communications and supply bases has been accompanied by its use as an instrument of terror against entire populations. In Vietnam, the consequences of the strategic bombing program and the use of defoliants as well as napalm caused stress among some pilots. It also demonstrated the futility of military technology that demoralized and destroyed the very people it was supposed to protect. The robotization of warfare as practiced in Vietnam degraded the status of some aviators to that of mere functionaries obeying instructions by a vast, remote bureaucracy. Boyne and Thompson (1986:437) perfectly catch the depressing effect this new status had on the morale of B-52 pilots carrying out strategic bombing missions with the complaint that their lives were being squandered, if not in casualties, then in boredom by "precisely controlled nonsense, a parody of warfare" in which command and control were exercised by means of new and extraordinary communications systems.

Among U.S. aviators in Vietnam, catch cries like "Two, four, six, eight! Who're we gonna defoliate?" (Lansdale 1976) and the song "Strafe the Town" sung by pilots at Ubon, a USAF base in Thailand, to the tune of "Wake the Town" (Broudy 1969; Fish 1989; Getz 1986a; Lansdale* 1976; Tuso 1990) were cries of moral conscience in the guise of black comedy.

> Strafe the town and kill the people!
> Burn their houses to the ground!
> Drop your naplam in the schoolyard!
> See the kiddies scurry round! Etc.

"Number One Clismas Song" (Getz 1981; Tuso 1971 and 1990) parodies "The Christmas Song" by inverting conventional, seasonal sentiments of peace and goodwill so that they become a cynical message of destruction directed at helpless civilians by technicians trapped in the machinery of violence. The pilot drops napalm on cripples limping down the street and wishes "Dear Ho" a "Melly Clismas."

The guilty cynicism and nervous laughter of the warrior are contrary to the general treatment of death by the popular culture which depicts it as a solemn sacrifice rather than as a subject for comic defiance or morbid humor. This is especially evident in the industry of ceremonial reverence with which the casualties from past wars are enshrined in war memorials and military cemeteries and commemorated in museums, parades, memorial days and ceremonial enactments and celebrations. So widespread and familiar are the icons of the historic military past that they are an important means by which the ordinary citizen in peacetime experiences the concept of war and contemplates its mortal implications in ways that do not violate society's assumptions about the patriotic duty of the warrior to serve his or her country in battle whenever crisis requires it, if necessary at the sacrifice of life itself.

The belief in sacrifice as an inevitable requirement for the collective redemption of group, community, state, nation and humankind is a central doctrine of Christianity that has been deeply implanted in Western culture. It postulates that the war dead sacrifice their lives in order that others might live, whatever reservations and profane comments they might personally make about the necessity for this sacrifice at the time. Their demise is given spiritual endorsement by burial rites, commemorative services and memorials that are part of a system of sacred belief about death that justifies and exalts the suffering and sacrifice of the mortal warrior. The supreme symbol of this sacrificial dedication emerged at the conclusion of World War 1 in the form of the Unknown Soldier.

The inspiration for this memorial may have owed something to the American Civil War. The carnage on some of its battlefields was such that, at the end of hostilities, thousands of unburied corpses still lay where they had fallen and special efforts had to be made to dispose of them. Arlington (which had formerly been the estate of the Confederate General Robert E. Lee) was declared a national cemetery, and interments began there. About 100 yards from Arlington House (Lee's former residence and now a museum) is a mass grave of 2,111 soldiers of the Civil War whose identities could not be established. An inscription on a memorial tombstone reads:

Beneath these stones repose the bones of two thousand one hundred and eleven unknown soldiers gathered after the war from the fields of Bull Run and the route to the Rappahannock. Their names could not be identified, but their deaths are recorded in the archives of their country and its grateful citizens honor them as of their noble army of martyrs. May they rest in peace. September A.D. 1866.

At the conclusion of World War 1, some of the participatory nations constructed monuments in which they carefully interred selected, representative specimens of their unidentified dead. The Arlington National Cemetery now contains a tomb housing an American unknown from each of World War 1, World War 2, the Korean War and the Vietnam War. An Honor Guard on duty 24 hours a day attracts large streams of visitors and sightseers. There are now over 200,000 graves in Arlington

Cemetery, and about 4,000 funerals take place there each year, some of them involving the drama of full military honors. This requires a horse-drawn caisson for the casket, a military band, an escort of troops, pall-bearers, a firing squad, a bugler and a chaplain.

As cultural production, the spectacular performance of such burial rites, the ceremonies at the tomb of the Unknown Soldier and the various observances conducted elsewhere in the cemetery are part of an elaborate system of symbols that dramatizes the fate of the warrior in a carefully contrived landscape of death. It is the scene for the enactment of sacred rituals that justify the warrior's sacrifice and at the same time confirm and exalt the nation's collective beliefs.

The rituals associated with this system of symbols are what Kenneth Burke (1954) has described as a drama of redemption in which the maintenance of social order requires the ritual sacrifice of appropriate victims. The war dead are perfect for this role because they have offered up their lives for the well-being of society, which redeems itself by their sacrifice and so becomes the more unified, integrated and reassured against the anxieties aroused in wartime.

The Arlington National Cemetery is part of a larger symbolic array of national institutions in Washington, D.C., that includes both the Lincoln and Vietnam memorials. The parts of this loosely coupled system are in reasonably close physical proximity and are a major attraction to the many thousands of tourists as well as American visitors to the Mall and its complex of museums and federal government organizations. Warner (1959:272–73) in his study of Memorial Day sees Lincoln as the most powerful of American collective representations, partly because he symbolizes the equalitarian ideal of the common man as well as the ability to rise from obscurity to greatness, and partly because of his sacrifice to an assassin's bullet "on the altar of unity, climaxing a deadly war."

Significantly, the Vietnam Memorial adjoins the Lincoln Memorial and, as a shrine that commemorates the sacrifice of some 58,000 American troops, performs a similar integratory function. It accommodates tensions about the meaning of the Vietnam War in such a way that the living can feel that the sacrifice of the dead has some tangible purpose. This is an important symbolic achievement because of the divisive state of popular opinion concerning U.S. involvement in Vietnam and the feeling of many Vietnam veterans that their sacrifices and sufferings were unappreciated[35] and that they themselves were outcasts and scapegoats.

Military museums, historic battlefields, memorials, reenactments of famous battles and public displays of military hardware and skills are a familiar attraction throughout America. Many of them are accompanied by what James Coombs (1989:72–73) calls "rituals of veneration." These give shape to a desired collective experience (e.g., sentimental or reverent feelings and gratifications concerning particular objects, buildings, events and people from the past) and may also (as in the case of war memorials and battlefield sites) impart a degree of sacred status to what is being venerated. A visit to Gettysburg, Arlington or the Vietnam Memorial is more than an indulgence in the cult of history, it is an experience that is just as sacred as participation in a formal religious service. Behind such secular shrines loom whole armies of the dead and the gigantic industry of a series of wars.

The controversial history of the Vietnam Memorial Wall and the struggles of the Vietnam veterans' movement to gain public acceptance are yet another illustration of the socialization function of popular culture and its capacity to deal with disturbing or disruptive experience. As a focus for emotional expression, the Wall has succeeded in transcending the wrangling over American participation in the war as well as the bitterness and recrimination over the failure of its objectives and the humiliation felt by many veterans at their public postwar reception.

NOTES

1. Collected in Chatham County, North Carolina, in 1923. Western Kentucky.

2. Obscure. Perhaps the name of a manufacturer of artificial limbs, or possibly the name of a surgeon at Oaklands Park Military Hospital, Surrey, England, where this song (from the Cleveland Collection) was current among World War 1 amputees.

3. Australian Imperial Force Headquarters near Victoria Station in London during World War 1. The soldier on leave, or being posted, had to go to three places on his arrival from France. One was to get his leave pass, travel warrants and other documents; the second was to call at the stores to draw a new kit or to have deficiencies made up; and the third was probably to draw pay. In order to avoid retracing his steps, he would be most likely to go straight to Horseferry Road and thence to other places. This would explain the disheveled condition of his tunic. In making this explanation (correspondence, 29 December 1975), Mick Shepherd also noted that an alternative usage was "Hawkesbury Road." Hawkesbury is a place in New South Wales well known to Australian soldiers and therefore an easy substitution as the song passed verbally from man to man.

4. A bludger was originally a prostitute's bully, but in Australian slang it came to mean anyone who does not earn an honest living or does not do his or her fair share of work. During World War 2, New Zealand infantry considered anybody not actually in the frontline to be a bludger, regardless of whatever functions they might be performing. The site of 2NZEF rear headquarters on a slight rise in Maadi Camp in the suburbs of Cairo was known contemptuously as "Bludgers' Hill."

5. To see all the parasites who practice their ingenious evasions and schemes for self-preservation and advancement." Alternatively, "Who dodge all the

strafe" (Shepherd to Cleveland, 29 December 1975). Strafe is a World War 1 term for artillery bombardment.

6. Australian slang: "truly," "emphatically."

7. "Lousy" is Australian slang for some person or situation that is unsatis-factory, disgusting, objectionable or unfair.

8. Both British and ANZAC troops in World War 1 wore service dress tunic and trousers. This uniform was replaced by battledress in World War 2.

9. Alternatively, Lahey (1965) and Ward (1964): "You look so disgraceful that people will laugh." The version reproduced in Edwards (1973) has a military policeman instead of a Lance-Corporal who says, "I'll just have to cancel your 14 days leave."

10. A light shell fired at close range from one of the smaller artillery pieces.

11. Field Marshal Gort (Sixth Viscount) served in the Grenadier Guards dur-ing World War 1, was a captain in 1914 and brevet major in 1916. He became a battalion commander, gained experience as a staff officer and also received the Victoria Cross. According to Shepherd, he was probably stationed at Horseferry Road for a very brief time during World War 1 in some comparatively junior capacity before returning to France. By the 1930s, he had become com-mander-in-chief of the British forces, and on the outbreak of World War 2, he went to France in command of the British Expeditionary Force. The reference to Lord Gort in the concluding stanza of the song has confused some writers. For instance, Cray (1992:403–4) thinks the text must have been written in 1940 because of Lord Gort's role in the debacle in France. But this is to ignore the fact that there were no Australian or New Zealand troops in that episode and that the Horseferry Road location of the Australian Imperial Force headquarters dates unmistakably from World War 1. There is a simple explanation for Lord Gort's presence there, and it is clear that the song originated in World War 1 among soldiers in the Australian and New Zealand Army Corps (ANZAC) which fought in France. It is a piece of Australian and New Zealand folklore transmitted through the professional armies of both countries to the World War 2 generation of 1940s soldiers.

12. Ward (1964:168). A romantic, frontier ethos that attributed manly virtues and the collective strengths of mateship to the predominantly male inhabitants of the vast Australian outback.

13. Ward (1964:232). See also Gammage (1974:37). "We are a free men, used to living a free life, with very few restraints of any kind, recognizing no one as Master...." A comment by an Australian soldier in 1915.

14. Archive of American folksong, LC. Collected in Teddington (near Lon-don) in 1944 from a petty officer in the British navy who heard it sung on a minesweeper based on Sousse (North Africa) in 1943.

15. Cleveland Collection.

16. The red light district in wartime Cairo.

17. Names of well-known Cairo prostitutes in World War 2.

18. Slang: "ten piastres," equivalent to about 1 shilling (or 10 cents) in 1940.

19. Arabic: "money."

20. "You could get a good position in the brothel queue."

21. Slang: "shite hawk" was the name given to the Indian whistling kite, a large, black, crowlike bird that scavenged around rubbish dumps.

22. A good quality light ale sold in Egyptian bars.

23. Page mistakenly attributes it to the tune of the "Eton Boating Song."

24. Page attributes it to the tune of "The Red River Valley," but the text is obviously a variant of the Benghazi, out-on-the-desert, banks-of-the-Imjin cycle.

25. Interviewed by the writer in 1986, a former soldier from the NZ Infantry Regiment which had been stationed in Taiping (between Kuala Lumpur and Penang) said the lyric originated in the battalion at that time. "A Maori corporal used to sing it and we joined in the final chorus." The last performance he heard was in the Sergeants Mess in Burnham Military Camp, New Zealand, in 1974. The text given here is from the Cleveland Collection.

26. Many of the company came from the East Coast of the North Island of New Zealand and were either related to the Maoris of that district or had close associations with them, as well as some knowledge of Maori traditions and language. Buck (1949:456) explains that *Tu* has several titles that include *Tukariri* (*Tu*-the-angry) and *Tukanguha* (*Tu*-the-enraged). The Angry Man is presumably an idiomatic Europeanization of these titles.

27. Underwood Collection. Current in the USAF in 1944.

28. Western Kentucky (Wilgus Collection).

29. Vietnam Veterans' Oral Archive, Buffalo. Collected by David M. Watt of Arlington, Tennessee.

30. Loc. cit.

31. The melody is "Dance of the Hours" from the opera *La Gioconda* by Amilcare Ponchielli. The words are a parody of "Hello Muddah, Hello Fadduh! (A Letter from Camp)" in an Alan Sherman LP recording made in the early 1960s.

32. 8 March 1988, Channel 5, Washington, D.C.

33. Gordon "Inferno," LC. Sung by field artillerymen "from 1917 to the present time," according to the informant. See also Dolph* 1929.

34. The reference to "the Pirate" is obscure. Perhaps it was contemporary argot for the German Navy, since its unrestricted warfare policy in World War 1 led to it being accused of piracy. Bracketing is a range-adjusting procedure in which shells fired at a target are gradually brought accurately to bear on it by raising and lowering the elevation of the gun or guns until the shots are falling correctly.

35. Deborah Ballard-Reisch (1991), in an analysis of recent television treatments of the Vietnam War, traces a process of redemption by which the Vietnam veteran, after being a scapegoat for the guilt felt by American society, is now encountering a fuller understanding and acceptance in a "national process of healing."

7

The Vietnam Warrior

The popular songs of the Vietnam War era had an ideological duality that mirrored the confusion in the homeland over the justification for the war and for its continuance. In its early phases, the conflict was defined in a series of releases, mostly in the country-western style, as a righteous crusade for freedom by heroic U.S. soldiers helping their South Vietnamese allies. An outstanding example of this perspective was Barry Sadler's "Ballad of the Green Berets," a 1964 hit in praise of fearless fighting men from the sky, while Merle Haggard's "Okie from Muskogee" (a 1969 hit) described the occupants of small-town America as righteous citizens who valued freedom and disapproved of the burning of draft cards.

By then, however, the war had inspired a torrent of protest by a vociferous peace movement. Many of its songs contained an indigenous vitality that was reminiscent of the Civil War period. Contemporary popular music was once again related directly to the passions and anxieties of an entire generation of people to the point where, in the hands of the peace movement, it became a political weapon. It augmented the techniques of protest and demonstration whereby masses of people could be indoctrinated, confirmed in their loyalties to a cause and set in motion against the targets for their anger and alarm.

Resistance to the war and to the consequences of being drafted intensified as the nature of the conflict emerged vividly on television news, as the casualties mounted and as it became increasingly evident that victory by the U.S. forces was improbable. Some protest songs made use of familiar, traditional airs. For instance, "The National Interest March" was composed to the tune of "The Battle Hymn of the Republic," but it objected to the flower of the country's youth "marching straight to hell."

The troops in Vietnam had ready access to tape recorders, stereo decks, music played by Filipino rock bands and broadcasts from the Armed Forces Network. A chain of stations featured 24-hour AM and FM broadcasting. Listeners wanted, above all, to hear about home and requested numbers like Porter Wagoner's "Green Grass of Home," Simon and Garfunkel's "Homeward Bound," Bobby Bare's "Detroit City" (with its dominant theme, "I wanna go home") and Peter, Paul and Mary's "Leaving on a Jet Plane." "Blowing in the Wind" went on air, even though it was regarded officially as unpatriotic, but there was trouble over Freda Payne's "Bring the Boys Home," which advised the troops to turn their ships around and lay their rifles down.[1]

Troops could bring in their own tapes and from varied sources were exposed to the antiwar sentiments of the peace movement, especially from the mid–1960s onward, in the music of songwriters and performers like Bob Dylan ("Masters of War" and "A Hard Rain's A-Gonna Fall"); Tom Paxton ("The Talkin' Vietnam Pot Luck Blues"); Phil Ochs ("Talkin' Vietnam Blues," "The Draft Dodger Rag" and "I Ain't Marchin' Anymore"); Arlo Guthrie ("The Alice's Restaurant Massacree"); John Prine ("Your Flag Decal Won't Get You into Heaven Any More"); and Country Joe and the Fish ("The I-Feel-Like-I'm-Fixin'-to-Die Rag"). As songs about the attractions of peace proliferated, the sounds of psychodelic rock also questioned a conformist approach to the war with their advocacy of flower-power, drugs and escapist fantasy.

As a source of oppositional ideology, songs like the Animals' "We Gotta Get Out of This Place" may have contributed to the demoralization of some of the troops in Vietnam. The military command was unable to control the mass media sufficiently to screen out the dissident sounds of protest. It was not even able to suppress the transmissions of illegal broadcasters operating from some of the major U.S. bases, making derisory comments about the war and playing hard rock. In such ways, the Vietnam warrior was exposed to contradictions about the perception of the war that could not be resolved even in the postwar period when veterans found themselves striving for recognition and acceptance. "Together Then, Together Again," a post–Vietnam lyric sung by Linda Jordan at a veterans' concert in Washington, D.C., in November 1984, summarized their predicament at not having a ticker tape parade or any "words of accolade."

Not everyone who served in Vietnam was in combat or faced a life of fear and danger. A modern Western army requires a large tail of logistical, administrative and various specialized, supporting services. In

1967, at the peak of the U.S. effort in Southeast Asia, over half of those drafted to Vietnam were in noncombat roles. Consequently, the superiority that all frontline soldiers feel toward rear-echelon staff emerged with familiar emphasis. Hershel Gober (a U.S. infantry officer working as an adviser in the Delta, and a talented musician and singer who later toured Vietnam with an entertainment group called the Black Patches) composed a satire about the "Saigon Warrior" in which he described how this comic figure could be recognized any day by his Australian bush hat with a Vietnam patch on the side, his low-slung six-gun and maybe a *Ba Muoi Ba* patch on his arm[2] as he helped to fight a war by pushing a pencil.

The classic statement of the frontline soldier's resentment toward those in the rear (no matter how dedicated or essential they might be) is contained in "The Lousy Lance-Corporal," already cited in the previous chapter. Australians who fought in Vietnam had a topical variant[3] of this (referred to in the following discussion as "Saigon Warrior II").

A trooper came down on his fourteen days leave
When up stepped a provost saying "Leave passes please,
There's blood on your tunic and guts on your sleeve,
I think I'll just cancel your fourteen days leave."

Chorus:

Dinky-die! Dinky-die!
I wouldn't, I couldn't not tell you a lie

The Trooper just gave him a murderous look,
Said: "See here you bastard I'm fresh from Hiep Duc
Where whizz-bangs are flying and comforts are few
And brave men are dying for bastards like you."

Dinky-die! Etc.

Oh Quang Ngai! Oh Quang Ngai!
A hell of a place,
The way things are done it's a fucking disgrace,
With Captains and Majors and Light Colonels too,
With their heads up their asses and nothing to do.

Dinky-die! Etc.

They stand in the compound,
They scream and they shout,
Of a whole lot of shit they know nothing about.
For all they accomplish they might as well be
Shoveling up shit in the South China Sea.

Dinky-die! Etc.

I fought in Ha Tahn,
I've fought up in Hue,
I've fought in this place for a year and some days,
And while you were down on the fat of your ass,
I was out at Kam Duc near the Ho Chi Minh Track.

Dinky-die! Etc.

Did you ever a father, did it ever occur?
Did you ever a mother and did you strike her?
When women have babies they have them with ease,
When harlots have babies they call them MPs.

Dinky-die! Etc.

A further verse was added in 1971 during the wind-up of American involvement in the I Corps area.

Oh the rules of engagement are something else too,
You can't shoot a dink unless he shoots at you,
For all of the murders we'd like to commit,
We end up with footprints all over our dick!

"Saigon Warrior II" is an example of the telescoping of two familiar lyrics inside the framework of a well-known tune. Both lyrics are part of an Australian and New Zealand tradition of military folklore. The two countries have long-standing defense arrangements based originally on their joint participation in an Anzac Army Corps in World War 1. Their common interests have led them into a series of alliances and cooperative undertakings that were strengthened by their experiences in World War 2 and maintained throughout the postwar Malayan Emergency, the Korean War and the Vietnam War. Both countries sent troops to Vietnam where they operated under the command of an Australian Task Force.

The two verses about Quang Ngai in "Saigon Warrior II" are an insertion derived from another World War 2 song that circulated in New Zealand and Australia and was also sung to the tune of "Villikins and His Dinah." This was a derogatory complaint about the training methods in base camps. The version given here is entitled "Waiouru's a Wonderful Place."[4] For Waiouru [pronounced Wy-oo-roo], any isolated and unpleasant military place name in either Australia or New Zealand could easily be substituted.

Oh they say that Waiouru's a wonderful place,
But the organization's a fucking disgrace;
There's bombardiers, sergeants and staff sergeants too,
With their hands in their pockets and fuck-all to do;

And out on the bull ring they yell and they shout;
They scream about things they know fuck-all about,
And for all that I learned there I might as well be
A-shoveling up shit on the Isle of Capri.

"Saigon Warrior III," sung to the same tune, repeats the criticism of people on the staff "with their hands in their pockets and nothing to do," and then ridicules the self-importance of the "Saigon Commando." After each verse, it introduces a choral couplet that has been adapted from "The Lousy Lance-Corporal." The phrase *dinky dau* [Vietnamese for crazy] is a melodic approximation of the original antipodean "dinky-die." The version that follows was sung by a woman visitor (thought to be an Australian journalist, or possibly a nurse) at a group singing competition held at Nha Trang, the headquarters of the U.S. 17th Aviation Group, in April 1967. It is one of the items on a tape recording of the Merrymen (Broudy* 1967).[5] A text is also reproduced in Broudy (1969) and, a sung version is included in In Country* (1991).

Saigon, oh Saigon's a wonderful place,
But the organization's a God-damn disgrace,
There are Captains and Majors and Light Colonels too,
With their hands in their pockets and nothing to do.

Chorus:

Singing *dinky dau, dinky dau, dinky dau* doo,
With their hands in their pockets and nothing to do.

Oh they sit at their desks and they scream and they shout,
And they talk of the war they know nothing about,
Against the VC they're not doing too well,
But if cordite were paper we'd be all blown to hell!

Oh a Saigon Commando's an unusual sight,
He wears his fatigues thought he's not in the fight;
A knife and a pistol his daily motif,
But you'll find him for lunch at the *Cercle Sportif!*[6]

The song continues with an account of how most Saigon commandos are wearing the Bronze Star which they got for writing reports about the war and not for getting shot at. Then it concludes:

When this war is over and you all go home,
You'll meet Saigon Warriors wherever you roam,
You'll know them by sight and they're not in your class,
They don't have diarrhoea, just a big chairborne ass!

The American advisers working with Vietnamese groups were known as the *Co Van My.* Such large numbers were engaged in tasks like combat training, working with Vietnamese units in the field or taking part in the Civil Operations and Revolutionary Development Support (CORDS) program that they inevitably became a target for satire. "The Ballad of the Co Van My" (Fish 1989), sung to the tune of "The Wabash Cannonball," poked fun at the adviser who could "play a thousand parts from a deadly jungle killer to a patron of the arts." A K-bar is a combat knife. Chu Lai was a major Marine Corps base on the South China Sea coast in Quang Tin province.

> He's got a leather pistol belt and a fake Australian cap
> Festooned with pins and badges, and a plastic-covered map;
> He wears a K-bar on his hip that he swopped for at Chu Lai,
> And his moustache curls beside his nose almost up to his eyes. Etc.

Musically, the Vietnam War can be seen as an outcropping of the folk-ballad revival of the 1960s with its flood of long-playing records and its festivals, sing-ins, hootenannies and concerts that made folk culture into a profitable big business. This featured the output of groups like the Weavers, the Song Spinners, the Limeliters, the Kingston Trio and Peter, Paul and Mary, and it brought performers like Joan Baez, Pete Seeger and Bob Dylan before enthusiastic audiences on a global scale.

An important consequence of all this activity was that many people were inspired to learn to play a musical instrument and to sing traditional and other melodies for themselves and their friends. The basis of popular culture was greatly expanded by the inclusion of this traditional repertoire. It was facilitated by Japanese and American industry which mass-produced good quality guitars, pianos and wood instruments at affordable prices. Many of the young Americans who were drafted for service in Vietnam were the direct beneficiaries of this cultural production, being able to play guitar, banjo, harmonica or some other instrument, often with professional skill. As in World War 2, those who were singers were always assured of an audience, even though entertainments in the field were much extended by record players, transistorized radios, the broadcasts of the Armed Forces Radio and Television Network in Vietnam (AFVN), as well as the activities of clandestine broadcasting stations that operated illicitly in barracks and military bases. Propaganda broadcasts could be received from Radio Hanoi, and comments could be exchanged over the "bullshit net" operated by some troops themselves on their field radios.

Portable tape records were available and were especially important in taping, learning and rapidly circulating a new song or a concert program. The range of possible dissemination of tape recordings was extended by the massive use of air transport in a mobile war that had no fixed frontlines. Troops could be moved about with flexibility, while performing groups could be flown from one location to another. In this way, a song featured by a group could spread around the base camps, airbases and other sites.

Knowledge of what was being sung in Vietnam owes much to the existence some twenty or more years later of copies of aviation unit songbooks and privately circulated copies of tapes made at concerts and song sessions in the field. The Merrymen were one typical singing group who became well known. Others who performed at the concert at Nha Trang were the Bite and Strikers, the Beach Bums, the Intruders, the Four Blades, the Blue Stars and the Mohawks. As noted in footnote 5, the name Merrymen was part of an elaborate organizational metaphor used to identify the 173rd Assault Helicopter Company. Since their unit radio designation was "Robin Hood," their members became generally known as "the Robin Hoods." Their gunships were called the "Crossbows," and the company cantonment was set up in "Sherwood Forest" among the rubber trees of what had once been an experimental plantation.[7]

Most of these field performers made extensive use of musical parodies derived either from the contemporary folk revival or from the country-western and rock music that was in wide circulation. Others were anchored in a continuous services tradition that had been inherited from the Korean War and World War 2, or in a few cases, even earlier. They made use of familiar, workhorse tunes like "Sweet Betsy from Pike" and "The Yellow Rose of Texas," as well as a repertoire of cowboy lyrics and hymn tunes that were part of the popular culture of the mid-twentieth century.

Some of these songs were critical of the war and those who supported its continuation. A parody of "The Caissons Go Rolling Along" (Berkeley), collected in 1969, was sung by one group of soldiers in Vietnam, usually in bars, "to indicate the feelings of a majority of U.S. troops toward the army and the war in general." A lifer is a professional volunteer, signified by R.A., meaning Regular Army.

Over hill, over dale, as we hit the dusty trail,
As the lifers go stumbling along,
Watch them drink, watch them stink,
Watch them even try to think,
As the lifers go stumbling along.

For it's heigh, heigh hee! Truly fucked are we!
Shout out your numbers loud and strong. R!A!
For wher'er you go, you will always know
That the lifers go stumbling along,
Stumble! Stumble! Stumble!

A parody of "I Want a Girl" (Berkeley), said to have been popular in the same informant's unit in Vietnam in 1965, expressed some bitterly ironic attitudes toward war in general.

> I want a war, just like the war
> That mutilated dear old Dad;
> It was the war, and the only war
> That Daddy ever had;
> A good old-fashioned war
> That was so cruel,
> But we all abided by Geneva rules
> HEY! (come in with gusto)
> I want a war, just like the war
> That mutilated dear old Dad.

A major source of information about the songs of the Vietnam War is located in the tape recordings collected by Major General Edward G. Lansdale. His is probably the first systematic use of tape recordings in wartime to collect songs and to use them for intelligence purposes. Lansdale served in military intelligence in World War 2 and was afterward transferred to the Philippines where he advised the Philippine Army on the reorganization of its intelligence services. By 1950 he had become a personal friend of Ramon Magsaysay, the secretary of defense who was later to become president. Lansdale assisted in putting down the Hukbalahap rebellion (a Communist-inspired agrarian movement) by developing a program of psychological warfare backed up with civic measures that advocated the rehabilitation of prisoners and a range of social, political and economic reforms to accompany the appropriate military action. The essential doctrine in all this was that Communist insurrection could only be successfully opposed by a combination of democratic reform with orthodox military counterinsurgency measures.

There was nothing original about such doctrine, but Lansdale's method of implementation had some unusual features. It depended on establishing a milieu in which people of different nationalities and backgrounds could mingle and socialize informally. The idea was to build up trust between the foreign representatives of counterinsurgency power and the leadership of the host country under threat. It was hoped that sensitive views and information could be gathered and exchanged on a basis of personal trust, and that in this way, the potential leaders for a new democratic order could be influenced and encouraged. Lansdale's technique was to use song sessions and hospitality as a confidence-building medium and as an instrument of political communication in the effort to consolidate stable forms of democratic government under leaders with whom the West, and the United States in particular, could cooperate.

In Vietnam, Lansdale encouraged composers, performers, musicians and friends to frequent his house at 194 Cong Ly in Saigon and to express themselves with informal freedom. The model for this was probably the "coffee Klatsch" sessions he used to hold in Manila while working there as an adviser in 1950. Among the visitors to his Saigon salon were personal friends in the military, members of the Senior Liaison Office (SLO) staff, people in the U.S. Foreign Service, the U.S. Information Agency, the Central Intelligence Agency, as well as prominent Vietnamese politicians, folksingers and musicians. The proceedings were informal and flexible. When Radio Hanoi announced a "hate America" week in 1965 and threatened to assassinate Lansdale, a street party was held at which Pham Duy (a Vietnamese composer and folksinger) and a variety of other people played and sang. One of them was Sergeant Roger Hopkins who just wandered in when he heard the music as he passed by. He contributed a number of items to the program.[8]

In 1967 Lansdale used recordings of some of the songs presented at these occasions to compile a tape-recorded report from the liaison team to his superiors.[9] Copies of this tape were sent to the U.S. ambassador in Saigon, to General William C. Westmoreland (commander of the U.S. Military Assistance Command, Vietnam) and to President Lyndon Johnson, Vice-President Hubert Humphrey, Defense Secretary Robert S. McNamara, Secretary of State Dean Rusk and other officials in Washington, D.C. The object was to impart a greater understanding of "the political and psychological nature of the struggle to those making decisions."[10]

This use of a mixture of occupational and popular song as a means of presenting sensitive policy making advice was a most unusual way of transmitting intelligence. The presentation contained narrative ballads by Vietnamese as well as American singers to illuminate idealistic aspects of the relationship between U.S. officials and peasants in the fields that were difficult to put into prosaic, official language. There were items by Pham Duy and several other Vietnamese performers. Others were sung by Hershel Gober and Jim Bullington (who had been a Foreign Service officer stationed in Hue). The main thrust of this material was to emphasize the ideal of cooperation and friendship between American advisers and the Vietnamese population. The songs sung by the Vietnamese consisted of worksongs, children's songs, a number of lyrical compositions about building a new hamlet and planting rice, as well as some propaganda survivals from the Viet Minh campaigns of 1945 against the French. These were items like "Guerrilla March," "Winter for the Fighting Man," and "Carrying the Paddy for the Soldiers." In more romantic terms, "The Rain on the Leaves," sung as a duet by Pham Duy and Steve Addis, an American folksinger who made a tour of Vietnam in 1964 under the auspices of the United States Information Agency

(USIA), spoke of the rain on the leaves as the tears of joy of a girl whose lover returns from the war.

Lansdale has been described as "a superb accidental folklorist" (Fish 1989). His collecting had an immediate, military purpose, and his main talent as a strategic impresario was to assemble presentations of popular culture and folksong that were illustrative of his ideological aims. As an experiment in socialization, the material he compiled in his 1967 tape was intended to "teach" his political masters that their big-war and search-and-destroy tactics were misconceived and that nothing short of a gigantic, integrative, hearts-and-minds exercise could win the war against communism.

The Vietcong used a variety of simple, morale-building propaganda songs that had wide circulation throughout Vietnam. The Senior Liaison Office (SLO) team recognized their inspirational power and sought to make use of similar material. A discussion between Lansdale, Pham Duy, some of the SLO staff and one of the ministers in President Ky's cabinet raised the possibility of using songs to reinforce the objectives of the pacification program. It was thought that a training cadre at Vung Tau could be taught songs that contained inspirational thoughts about Vietnam in which the most important theme would be that the people should make Vietnam strong and that they would have to stand up for themselves and fight the Vietcong.[11]

In 1976 Lansdale compiled another tape for archival purposes at his home in Virginia.[12] This contained some 169 items that span the period of U.S. involvement in Vietnam from 1965 to 1972. In addition to a number of commercial recordings by performers like Barry Sadler and Dick Jonas, it included songs by Gober, Bullington and Dolf Droge. These were augmented by items from the Merrymen and by choruses from the "Cosmos Command Choir."

The "Cosmos Command Choir" consisted of habitues of the Cosmos Bar, a small establishment behind the U.S. Embassy in Ham Nghi Street in Saigon. It was frequented at lunchtimes and in the evenings by the CIA staff at the Embassy. This gathering was entirely informal and had the advantage that people could meet and speak freely and unofficially. According to one member of this circle[13] the premises were used partly to unwind from the tensions of the job and also to find out what was going on, especially from field officers. The CIA staff wore civilian clothes and could not readily use other facilities around the city because they would have been too conspicuous. The camaraderie in the bar was great. It styled itself the Cosmos Command and had a mock shield, shoulder patches and insignia.

All this took on a somewhat ironic significance in view of the flow of satires and critiques of official U.S. policy in Vietnam that emanated from the song sessions held in the bar. It was thought that at times

Soldiers of the 173rd Airborne Brigade unloading supplies from a UH-1B Iroquois helicopter (the battlefield workhorse) in preparation for an operation in Vietnam, 9 May 1967. *(U.S. Army)*

Pallets loaded with mail for aerial re-supply to troops in the field in Vietnam, May 1967. *(U.S. Army)*

The 1st Infantry Division band in Vietnam, 1966. *(U.S. Army)*

A U.S. Marine
Corps group per-
forming at an
NCO's club in Viet-
nam. *(U.S. Army)*

Edward G. Lansdale (right) receiving the Distinguished Service Medal from General Nathan F. Twining, then Air Force Chief of Staff at a ceremony in the Pentagon, 8 January 1957. *(U.S. Army)*

Staff Sergeant Victor Kalicki playing a Vietnamese flute in an outpost on Black Virgin Mountain, Vietnam, 1965. *(U.S. Army)*

Washington was being denied an understanding of how things actually appeared in Saigon because reports from the ambassador were optimistic and selective. Certainly, the views emanating from the Cosmos Command and other critics, as they have been preserved in the Lansdale tapes, amount to a cynical demolition of many official illusions.

For instance, songs that deal with events from 1962–65 comment scathingly on the instability of political life in South Vietnam, especially the coups that accompanied the power struggles and intrigues of the period. To the tune of "Sioux City Sue," the Cosmos Command Choir sang about "a little coup" in Saigon, while its 1964 version of "Let's Do It" named a whole spectrum of South Vietnamese politicians as potential coup participants. The sinister Madame Nhu (sister of President Diem) was satirized (to the tune of "The Yellow Rose of Texas") as a clever adventuress who was able to delude the U.S. leadership into supporting her husband's interests. The role of the U.S. advisory teams and the optimism attached to the strategy of pacification in 1962–63 were briskly ridiculed in "Ghost Advisers By and By" (to the tune of "Riders in the Sky"). These were described as Yanks who went out advising in South Vietnam only to find that the people they advised "didn't give a damn." The song had the advisers telling the U.S. secretary of defense (Robert S. McNamara) that the war was in the bag, but forgetting to inform the omnipotent Vietcong. It concluded with the advisers fighting their way on to the planes at Ton Son Nhut, a major airbase on the outskirts of Saigon, in a surrealistic preview of the frantic exodus that was to ensue in 1975.

An important concept in the strategy of counterinsurgency as practiced in Vietnam was that each U.S. adviser should work with a counterpart in the South Vietnamese forces. This generated some amusement in the Cosmos Command with the song "Don't Take My Counterpart Away" to the tune of "You Are My Sunshine." By 1965 the satirists of the Command were expressing little confidence in the official optimism about the progress of the war. "We Are Winning" (to the tune of "Rock of Ages") questioned the truth of assertions by General Paul D. Harkins (U.S. commander in Vietnam from 1962 to 1964), Henry Cabot Lodge (the U.S. ambassador in Vietnam) and Robert S. McNamara, to the effect that the Vietcong were being defeated.

Other songs emanating from the Cosmos Command satirized the disparity between statistical methods of appraising the cost effectiveness of operations and the actuality of events on the ground. They also laughed at the inability of the U.S. Command to define clear strategic objectives. A parody of "Oh Dear, What Can the Matter Be?" sung by Dolf Droge, pointed out that there were "eighteen generals and still no strategy."

In the course of a lecture at a Marine Corps training school, Droge sang a parody of "The Marine's Hymn" in which he tried to explain the importance of the peasantry in the Vietnam conflict. It is a brilliant example of his improvisatory talent as well as an exposition of the fatal flaw in those counterinsurgency operations that only succeeded in destroying the peasants' livelihood and turning them into Vietcong sympathizers. It also vividly illustrated the essential argument being propounded by the Lansdale circle to the effect that the war would be won or lost in the minds of the peasantry.

> From the shores of the Perdinales
> We have come to fight VC,
> But to win you must remember
> Do not burn the banana tree,
> For the farmer leads a wretched life,
> Less than fifty bucks a year;
> Your napalm bomb he does not like,
> From his life you must remove fear;
> But if you burn huts and shoot buffalo,
> Just remember what it means,
> You are working then for Uncle Ho
> Not United States Marines.

Vietnam warriors were faced with intolerable conflicts. On the one hand, the official ideology of the military command exhorted them to heroic behavior and dedication to the mission. On the other hand, the confused strategic objectives of the war seemed unattainable, while field operations all too often resulted in devastation and suffering to the civilian population and precipitated moral crises about the righteousness of what was being done. The songs of Vietnam explore these contradictions just as they invoke the love of life and the fear of death. A conflict of values confronted the fighter pilot bombing and strafing villages or dropping "chocolate-covered napalm" on them. The intelligence analysts in the Cosmos Bar, aware that the war could not be won by the methods being employed and the political direction being imposed from Washington, also encountered a crisis of frustration and doubt. Such dissonant experiences and apprehensions needed acting out in a context of group expression.

Other considerations had a bearing on the production and circulation of songs by the troops in Vietnam. The increased mobility of helicopter-borne infantry, as well as the use of large transport planes to move troops in and out of the theater, may have reduced some of the opportunities for singing. There were few long voyages on troopships, although when there were, as in the case of the Merrymen, the familiar industry of self-entertainment soon asserted itself. Certainly, far less time was spent marching along roadways or waiting in transit camps for overseas drafts to assemble. The proliferation of electronic media meant that troops were exposed to the popular culture of the homeland in greater volume, especially its commercial music. However, the ability to make and circulate tape recordings meant that songs composed in the field could reach wide audiences more efficiently than by reliance on typescript or word of mouth.

In any case, media usage depended on the outfit. Illegal radio transmitters were operating around some of the bases and are thought by some commentators to have contributed to the demoralization that affected some units because of their reproduction of hard rock and protest songs that contained antiwar sentiments. For example, "Dave Rabbit," the disc jockey of an unauthorized station broadcasting in the Saigon–Phan Rang area, played acid rock interspersed with announcements about new brothels, warnings about "a pusher selling bad H" and aphorisms like "Army sucks" and "Fuck it before it fucks you."

According to one writer, "rock and roll defined Vietnam as well as any novel."[14] Donald Bodey (1985:207), in an account of life in the field with an infantry platoon, describes radios and cassettes going everywhere in a landing zone and everyone screaming out the chorus of a Rolling Stones number. However, outside the perimeter, troops with any common sense were too concerned with their personal security to risk their lives listening to radio entertainment. Lanning (1987:63), in his account of his experience as a platoon leader, warns against exaggerating the effects of radio broadcasts. Though REMFs (rear-echelon mother fuckers) could listen to radio or watch television at their leisure, the radio was a luxury people in the field could not afford because the noise was not conducive to finding the enemy.

The practice of rotation in Vietnam probably had a more damaging effect on the morale of the U.S. forces in general, but it did not stop the formation of entertainment groups in which composers could try out their songs. As the career of the Merrymen indicates, air force bases, officers' clubs and helicopter unit headquarters were a stable sanctuary for a regular, organized social life where instrumental groups could rehearse and gain access to appreciative audiences.

Tuso (1971 and 1990) describes the circumstances of composition for some of the hundreds of songs that circulated in Vietnam and Thailand. Songs locally composed and performed were central to the pilots' social life and were copied and taped again and again. Each base or squadron had its own composer.

Apart from interludes in barracks and hutments, the main sites for performances of the songs of army aviators were either unit officers' clubs where informal sessions could take place or at the social gatherings that accompanied regular commanders' conferences. The singing contest recorded in Broudy* (1967) was a festive affair involving pilots from units all over the region as well as their hosts at the 17th Aviation Group headquarters in Nha Trang. This was staged at their officers' club, known as the Cockpit Club. The pattern of performance was structured so that each group that had flown in for the occasion could give a formal presentation of its item. Ballot papers were distributed to the audience, and the group with the best score was declared the winner. The event was held in the evening and terminated about 11 P.M., after which the Merrymen presented a series of songs.

Two of the contesting groups had a country-western sound, but the majority relied on a musical style that imitated the 1960s folk-revival idiom as exemplified by groups like the Kingston Trio. One or more lead singers, sometimes in unison, sometimes in close harmony, were backed by one or more guitars. In expressive terms, the show was relatively restrained, probably because of the presence of a general as well as the group's commanding officer and one female guest who was deferred to throughout with awkward courtesy in the inclusive phrase "Lady and Gentlemen." Continuity depended on the talents of a master of ceremonies who was also the Group Headquarters medical officer. With the aid of a stage equipped with a microphone and sound system, he made jokes about the brass and wise-cracked his way through the evening like the host in a radio or television talent quest. He called people up from the audience and made phoney presentations, he read doggerel verses, and when an item was delayed, he filled-in himself with a soft-shoe dance and a parody of "The Ballad of the Green Berets" entitled "The Flying Eyes of G.I. Joe."

Most of the songs presented at the singing contest were concerned with the techniques of being a pilot and with the responsibilities it entailed. They reflected the philosophy of the happy warrior, doing his job and taking pride in his accomplishments, with occasional gestures of apprehension about the occupational hazards involved in combat flying. A few items contained inspirational testaments of belief in the mission. For instance, a spoken introduction to an item by the Merrymen stated that no matter how important their job might be as aviators, the most important thing was to support the man on the ground. They took him into battle, but they left him there and flew back to sleep in a warm bed at night. So they had written a song about "that boy, 18 years old, sitting in an outpost, ten thousand miles from the people he loves," and they called it "Not Alone Am I."

Notwithstanding such occasional tributes to the importance of the ordinary soldier, as a major source the available tapes and printed texts of songs from the Vietnam War suffer from a cultural bias. They do not contain many items sung by Grunts and even fewer performances or compositions by black soldiers, despite the existence in American folklore of a large body of songs that establish black music as what Levine (1977:246) calls "a central vehicle for the expression of discontent and protest" as well as a recognized tradition of folksong among black soldiers in World War 1.

An example of that tradition is evident in a pioneering collection of the improvisations of "these natural-born singers" made by John J. Niles (1927). It contained variants of "'I Want to Go Home'" work songs about "diggin' in France"; songs about slumgullion in the oven and coffee in the pot; the pleasures of getting back to Tennessee; a burial song about having "a grave-diggin' feeling in my heart"; and a song about "Crap Shootin' Charlie" ("come on bones and treat me nice").

If black soldiers in Vietnam wanted to express their feelings about their situation, they could also draw on extremely sensitive language registers of the kind spoken idiomatically in the streets of America. Samples of their informal modes of expression could perhaps have been gathered at field sites, but the interests of Lansdale and the few collectors who were active during the Vietnam War appear to have been directed to the more formal opportunities provided by song sessions at locations like Lansdale's house, the officers' clubs at USAF bases or concerts given by singing groups at unit headquarters. Such organized entertainments probably owed something to the college song tradition of the homeland as well as the 1960s folksong revival. They are compatible with a military version of middle-class culture in which officers are segregated from other ranks, are expected to refrain from obscenity and, at least in public, are supposed to regulate their conduct in accordance with service codes of honor, duty and good manners.

In contrast, the rank and file can resort to whatever uninhibited verbal play they choose. Glimpses of this alternative world of experience are evident in an unidentified vocalist growling out "The Bong Son Blues" ("you can have them for a dollar") and a sardonic exercise in self-parody entitled "We're Gonna Rape and Kill" in Scaff* (1987). Another tape recording (Almazol* n.d.) contains items that appear to have been re-corded at a gathering of Air Cavalry troopers. One of them is "The Great Big Loudmouth Mother Jumper." This is an adaptation of Little Richard in "Slippin' and Slidin' (Peepin' and Hidin')," a 1956 recording by Richard Peniman, a black entertainer from Georgia. The lyrics of the Vietnam version consist of a dialogue in which the singer asks questions like "Well, who's that great, big, red-necked, loudmouth over there?" These are answered by the same singer in a comic falsetto, using phrases like "Yeah, yeah, I know it's him" and "Let them bones roll!" The nar-rative describes the sexual ardors of courtship with vernacular phrases like "Baby I love your ass" and "Anyway you want me, let it roll." Then it concludes with an announcement that the object of desire, now seen as "a great big, loudmouth, mother jumper," is pregnant.

A narration included in Scaff* (1987) was originally recorded at a troop's social gathering in the northern Binh Dinh province of Vietnam in 1969. It is a version of one of the humorous monologues of Dave Gardner recorded in "Kick Thy Own Self" in 1960. However, it has qualities of expression that are denied the performers in more formal entertainments. The language is more colloquial and is much richer in narrative detail. It is a variant of the haunted house tale (Browne and Drake 1976) in which a rich man with a fine, but haunted, mansion offers a reward to anybody who will spend a night in it. A stranger agrees and is sitting in a rocking chair when a cat comes in and starts talking to him. The cat can be interpreted as an animal hero, or he may take on the significance of a "cool cat" or black male who triumphs by using wit and persuasion rather than physical force in the style described by Abrahams (1970b:87).

The Vietnam version of this tale is delivered in an imitation Afro-American idiom using the dramatic style of a toast in which the narrator introduces himself as "Joe Blow, the Kokomo." He takes his listeners through a sequence of comic events in which the stranger is warned that there is somebody called "the Mother Fucker" who will "scare your pants off." When the cat comes in, he behaves with aggressive defiance. The stranger asks him nervously if he is going to be there when the Mother Fucker comes around, but the cat replies: "I thought you *was* the Mother Fucker." (Laughter).

Such laughter is an echo from the expressive world of ordinary people in wartime. Popular culture helps them define the human capacity for patriotic idealism as well as laughter, cynicism and despair. It probes the mechanics of fear and explores the mysteries of life and death as it experiments with the relationships between the powerful and the powerless. These range from the enthusiastic collaboration of the happy warrior to the apprehension and discontent of the reluctant conscript or the disillusioned volunteer. But their oppositional qualities are not enough to change the arrangements that keep the powerless quiescent. In most armies, except in time of exceptional disorder or crisis, soldiers are no more able to bring about revolutionary change than American blacks were during the era of slavery. There is very little evidence that their spirituals or work songs precipitated any of the numerous slave revolts that preceded the Civil War, although a "restricted code" of communication may have been influential in consciousness raising and in complementing and encouraging resistance techniques such as strikes, incendiarism, malingering and the organization of escapes.

Perhaps soldiers in Vietnam who sang about the "freedom bird" and life back in "the World" and listened to the hard rock music of the counterculture were in a roughly comparable situation, except that, unlike the slaves, they had prospects of liberation at the end of their tour of duty, providing they survived. Those who sang "All My Trials Lord" may have had an approaching day of liberation specifically in mind as well as a general sense of entrapment in an oppressive situation, but there is nothing about such a song to excite immediate disaffection, unless a very great deal is read into its innocuous lyrics.

The powerlessness of people in the wartime services has some resemblance to the situation of the miners of the Appalachian Valley studied by John Gaventa (1980). The miners' attempts at protest and rebellion were insufficient either to confront power or to overcome the "accumulated effects of powerlessness" (Gaventa 1980:258). Protest songs may therefore have only a limited scope in dealing with specific issues or questions of policy, rather than on a grander scale trying to reform the military system or change the nature of political decision making. The Allied soldiers who sang parodies of "Lili Marlene" in their efforts to obtain speedier repatriation at the end of World War 2 were not concerned about their powerlessness so much as activated by the simple desire to get back home and obtain a discharge. The impatience of the reluctant warrior is more a relief valve than an explosive accelerant of rebellion. Its function may be largely symbolic.

This is supported by Jackson's observation (1972:30) about the singing of Texas penitentiary prisoners changing the nature of the work to which they were compelled by putting it into their own appreciative framework rather than that of the guards. It became their work, conducted at their rhythm. To the reluctant warrior grousing about life in the services, grumbling about the food or yearning for the comforts of home, the singing of oppositional songs offers a semblance of at least having some control over the dictates of technique in the performance of duties. "Fuck 'Em All" thus becomes a hymn of endurance and a source of psychological support as much as it is a disaffected denunciation of authority. Singing such songs is a resistance to the commodification and automation of soldiers and their transformation into obedient robots. It converts drudgery into a self-accepted and self-directed activity by means of the therapy of laughter, and it asserts what is perhaps the ultimate superiority of democracy as a survivalist philosophy. If you cannot change the way things are, at least you can indulge in your freedom to laugh at them, at your enemies and at your puny self.

The flood of popular music and parody that circulates in wartime can be understood both as a form of media-inspired play and an orchestration to warfare as a deadly kind of social game. It is played willingly, even enthusiastically, by some happy warriors, or with varying degrees of reluctance and resistance by less dedicated others. Many lyrics reinforce morale by maintaining sentimental and patriotic linkages with the homeland. Others help to bring fears and anxieties under social control, while an uninhibited core of less compliant utterance allows criticism and resentment of authority to be openly voiced within the boundaries of official tolerance as a desirable alternative to refusal of duty or even mutiny.

Popular culture is penetrated by many caricatures of warfare. In addition to the military component of the children's toy industry and the epic melodramas of videofilm and the movie industry, it has inspired some political movements as well as motor cycle gangs to wear old World War 2 German apparel, to decorate themselves with swastikas and to arm themselves with a miscellany of weapons. It also excites imitative currents of ludenic activity in the form of computerized war gaming, video parlor and computer games based on combat situations, shootouts in tag-war ranges, firearms and military souvenir collecting and exhibiting, rifle and pistol shooting, recreational hunting, the reading and collecting of war comics, the acquisition of battlefield memorabilia and the wearing of military surplus uniforms and equipment. Such diversions are both an indulgence in aggressive fantasies and an extension of juvenile play into peacetime adult life.

Like the expressive features of carnival, festival, mass sports and community celebrations, warfare itself contains a subworld of postchildhood play. The young soldiers who gambled, drank, played games, believed in Gremlins and lucky charms, sang nursery rhymes, performed the "Unlucky for Some" and "Gasmask" dances, as well as dressing in colorful scarves, exotic hats and nonissue T shirts, were instinctively humanizing their circumstances by adapting familiar varieties of urban recreation, amusement and play to the need to make the sinister and barbarous landscapes of the battlefields more bearable.

Such transformations lessen the cultural impoverishment of military frontiers. The conversion of their hostile wastelands into negotiated spaces in which the warriors can temporarily impose their own codes of play and entertainment makes them performers in a violent, historical theater that reenacts experience across the boundaries of time. The frontier heroics of this drama exploit the aggressive fantasies of Gunslingers, Wolf Packs, Grunts and Dogfaces as they directly relay one generation's folk experience to another.

Although war is a historical anachronism that threatens civilization, it is also, paradoxically, a cultural shelter for the renewal of such transgenerational experiences as well as a venue for traditional performance and composition in group contexts. Twentieth-century technological advances in commercial entertainment have made many areas of popular culture so subsidiary to the sponsorship of the electronic media industries that wartime now provides perhaps the only widespread milieu in which active group musical expression based on live performance can flourish on a large scale.[15]

Modern warfare is so interpenetrated by the popular culture of its participants that it can only be fully understood as one of popular culture's more violent and spectacular modes of operation. In this sense, war *is* popular culture. Its content reveals and helps resolve the contradictions that beset twentieth-century warriors. It registers their fears and doubts, but through music, entertainment, newspapers, television, radio, religious, postal, welfare and rest and recreational services it keeps reminding them of the homeland and its values and expectations. Wartime soldiers are essentially civilians temporarily transferred to the battlefields to consume such versions of popular culture as the military command think suitable or are unable to screen out. In this way, war and popular culture converge to keep the assembly lines of patriotic service working uninterruptedly and as enthusiastically as possible. Not just the singing warrior, but the entire nation, collaborate extensively in this enterprise, though not without reservation and apprehension.

War also galvanizes the popular culture into a frenzied output of descriptive journalism and patriotic exhortation. It excites the music, broadcasting, film and entertainment industries into a fever of crusading sentimentality, and it encourages the mobilization of people and resources not only for economic support of the war effort, but also for the performance of voluntary tasks. Wartime offers the civilian population glamorous excitements and personal gratifications that enable noncombatants to enlarge their lives by undertaking patriotic duties, helping to entertain troops and sharing in the general euphoria with which the popular culture responds to the challenge of hostilities.

War and military tradition are an emotional outlet for some of the expressive energies of popular culture. They generate images of sacred veneration, ceremonial solemnity, communal unity, anxiety, sacrifice, patriotism, heroism and comradeship, all orchestrated by popular music and song as well as the laughter and conviviality of the young. The varied forms of popular culture have a catalytic unity. They help propel people into wartime roles, and they inspire them with a hyperbole of heroism, sacrifice and patriotic effort. They also entertain them, provide for their welfare, impart dramatic styles of behavior to military life and smooth over the contradictions that emerge between idealism and actuality. At the conclusion of hostilities, the mediatory power of popular culture defines the relationships between the living and the dead and presides over their commemorative rites.

In spite of the tributes of mortality it exacts, and notwithstanding its savagery and wastefulness as a method for resolving conflicts, war is not entirely a negative and destructive force. Lloyd Warner (1959:274–78) points out that small-town and small-city Americans get their deepest satisfactions in time of war through a revitalized participation in social life, a heightened sense of individual significance and the excitement of sharing in the ideology of common sacrifice for the good of the country.

Repugnant though such a paradox might seem in view of the catastrophic potentialities of current military technology, popular culture has cohesive strengths that are important for collective survival.

The innate expressive wisdom of the total field of popular culture and its genius for making the best of things are dramatically exhibited in wartime. This may have a potential bearing on peacetime crisis attempts to deal internationally with famine, drought, disease, climate change, ecological damage and other disasters. To meet such threats to common survival, the world is being driven reluctantly along the pathways of increasing international cooperation both by anxious governments and by numerous voluntary agencies that depend on widespread public support and participation. Perhaps the integrative idealism of wartime popular culture needs to be applied more directly and purposefully to peaceful global projects. This could help make the world a healthier and safer place, especially if the processes of change were to be accelerated by the mobilizing and inspirational energies that popular culture displays so enthusiastically in the crises of wartime.

This creative element in popular culture is often overlooked or underestimated. Its comic vision turns disasters and sufferings into ironic laughter, but its romanticism offers a benign, integrative view of the possibilities of life. A curious foreshadowing of such constructive potentialities took place at the end of World War 2 in Europe. Everywhere, streams of refugees, displaced persons and soldiers trying to return to their homelands trudged along the highways, overloaded the few operational train services and begged for lifts on military transport. The whole of Europe was in labored movement, but the survivors of the battalion in which the present writer served were encamped in the grapevines around an airfield on the Adriatic coast of Italy. There they apprehensively awaited their future which, at that time, looked as though it might involve a move to the Asiatic front where the war against Japan was still in violent progress.

It was night time, and somebody had lit a fire from the remains of a shattered building. Soldiers attracted to it joined in a desultory attempt at a singsong. The mood was sombre, and the sound was ragged and uncertain as they drifted into a mournful rendering of "Lili Marlene." Suddenly an accession of new voices transformed the performance. The singers had been joined by a group of German prisoners of war from a nearby camp where they were awaiting repatriation. It was as if a fragment of disordered, homeless Europe had stumbled into a momentary coherence with the aid of a popular song that transcended borders, nationalities and ideologies by its sentimental power and simplicity. Under the influence of the most moving popular lyric of World War 2, a gathering of survivors improvised a few frail moments of transient community in spite of the legacy of hate and anger that still divided them.

It was to be nearly fifty years before any semblance of political and economic concord was to be even remotely realizable in Europe, but its tentative beginnings may have been implicit all along in its most familiar expressions of popular culture.

NOTES

1. See "When Rock Went to War," *Veteran*, Vol. 6, No. 2, Washington, D.C., February 1986.

2. *Ba Muoi Ba* is Vietnamese for the number thirty-three and also the brand name of a variety of bottled beer sold in Vietnam. It was known as "Tiger Piss" because of the tiger on the label.

3. The text cited here is from the Vietnam Veterans Oral Archive and Folklore Project at Buffalo. The informant, David M. Watt of Arlington, Tennessee, heard it in 1971 from Australians stationed at Chu Lai in an MACV team. Quang Ngai is a coastal town on Highway 1 about 75 miles south of Danang.

4. Waiouru is situated on a volcanic plateau among mountains in the center of the North Island of New Zealand. It was always regarded as the most isolated and desolate of all the wartime training camps. "The Isle of Capri" was the title of a romantic popular song hit of the 1930s. The bull ring is military slang for parade ground. The text is from the Cleveland Collection.

5. An account of the formation of the Merrymen is given in a tape (now held at the Vietnam Veterans Oral Archive and Folklore Project at Buffalo) which they recorded at the 173rd Assault Helicopter Company base at Lai Khe in December 1966. It explains that the original group was a trio formed on the USS *Walker* during the crossing to Vietnam. It consisted of Lieutenant Thomas (guitar), Captain Greg Chapman (percussion) and Captain Joe Drew (guitar). At Danang they met Lieutenant Mike Staggs of the 116th Aviation Company, and after several singing sessions he was transferred to become the fourth member of the group.

6. A fashionable club in Saigon.

7. According to a former staff officer stationed at Lai Khe, interviewed 21 April 1988.

8. These are recorded in the Lansdale Collection located in the Hoover Institution Archives at Stanford (tapes 7–10, dated 18 December 1965).

9. LWO 8281, LC. Duplicates are lodged in the Lansdale Collection in the Hoover Institute Archives at Stanford (tape No. 30).

10. Quoted in Fish (1989) as part of a commentary by Lansdale on the significance of his 1967 tape which he entitled "In the Midst of War." Fish (1989) also gives an account of the circumstances of its production.

11. Recorded in the Lansdale Collection, Hoover Institution Archives, Stanford (tapes 4–6, dated 25 November 1965).

12. Cited here as Lansdale (1976). This was entitled "Songs by Americans in the Vietnam War." A duplicate is in the Lansdale Collection at the Hoover Institution Archives, Stanford (tapes 62–67). An account of the compilation of the 1976 tape is given in Fish (1989). She reproduces an explanation that accompanied its deposition in the Library of Congress in which Lansdale stated

that the collection was given so that the songs would be available to all who were interested. They deserved presentation as insights into the feelings of the Americans who fought in the war and they should prove invaluable to the scholar or the historian seeking a true understanding of it. An unpublished catalogue of the content of Lansdale (1967 and 1976) with a transcription of the commentaries linking the various items, as well as a supporting bibliography, has been prepared by Lydia Fish as "Research Notes" and is lodged in the Vietnam Veterans Oral History and Folklore Archive at Buffalo.

13. A former intelligence analyst at the U.S. Embassy in Saigon, interviewed in Washington, D.C., 9 December 1987.

14. "When Rock Went to War in Vietnam," *Veteran*, Vol. 6, No. 2, February 1986.

15. Isolated frontier life is a similar male refuge for group singing and the transmission of folk material. A mimeographed songbook (Cleveland Collection) compiled by American and New Zealand personnel at Scott Base, Antarctica, in 1971 contains the texts of 117 songs and verses and ten prose narratives. Regular song sessions were held with its aid.

Appendix

Submarine Song

The battleships are mighty,
They're the backbone of the fleet;
The aircraft and destroyers
Are awfully hard to beat;
The battle cruiser squadron
Is known from sea to sea
But a good old greasy submarine
Is home sweet home to me.

Submarines nice,
Submarines twice,
Jolly jumping Jesus Christ!
Have I been on 'em?
I should smile,
I've been on 'em
For a hell of a while!

Tune: unknown
Source: Western Kentucky

We Walked Here
(Latrun, May 1941)

We walked here from Narvik,
You through Italy,
We from Czechoslovakia,

And many others from Syria.
Three escaped from Germany,
We through the sea,
And you through Flanders,
We through mountains,
You through forests.
Now altogether toward Alexandria,
We're together again.
Carpathian Brigade,
It's a big world
And the soldier is a homeless wanderer
Forever.

Source: Leo* (1944) (Present author's translation)

The Red Poppies of Cassino

Do you see those ruins on the summit?
Your enemy hides there like a rat.
You must! You must! You must!
Take him by the scruff of the neck
And thrust him from the clouds!
So they went with rage and anger
To slaughter and take revenge;
As always, they went strong-willed,
As always, to fight with honor.

Chorus:

The red poppies of Monte Cassino
Drank Polish blood instead of dew.
Soldiers walked through them and died,
But our anger was strengthened by these deaths.
Years will pass, centuries will go by,
But traces will remain of these former days
And all the poppies of Monte Cassino
Will be the redder because they will grow
From Polish blood.

Doom-laden, they charged through enemy fire,
And many were hit and fell.
Like the insane Samosierry,[1]
Like the ones from Rokitno,[2]
They ran on, driven by an insane impulse
And they got to their objective;
The attack was successful;
They placed their red and white banner[3]
In the ruins amongst the clouds.

Do you see the rows of white crosses?[4]
This Pole attained his death with honor;

Go forward! Go further! Go higher!
More you will find at your feet.
Now this land has become Polish soil
Although Poland is a long way off,
But Freedom's crosses are marred;[5]
This historical feat
Has but one defect.[6]

Source: The original Polish lyrics are by Feliks Konarski, and the melody is by Alfred Schutz. The English translation is by the present author.

The Soldier's Prayer

The Midnight Fusiliers

Eyes right! Fore-skins tight ass.-holes to the rear!

we're the boys who make no noise, we're al-ways full of

beer, we're the he-roes of the night and we'd

rath-er fuck than fight, we're the he-roes of the

Skin-back Fus-il-iers and the bud-ies of the skin-back

Gren-a-diers

Castel Frentano

There's a lit-tle vil-lage just be-yond the San-gro, Just a
vil-lage on a hill, And though we're ma-ny wea-ry
miles be-yond the San-gro, That's where my thoughts keep turn-ing still. Oh!
Cas - tel Fren - ta - no! Where the mon-ast-ery bells ring
out with do - ve va - do? But I'd ra - ther be there than in Mi -
la - no, Cas tel Fren - ta - no.

NOTES

1. Some 17,000 Polish soldiers served with the French armies during the Napoleonic Wars. Those who were in the Spanish peninsula campaigns of 1808–12 distinguished themselves by their bravery, especially at Somosierra on 30 November 1808. The capture of this place opened the road for the French troops to enter Madrid.

2. Rokitno was the scene of a famous battle in Polish history.

3. The Polish flag was a white eagle on a red background.

4. The military cemetery at Cassino.

5. By the Polish casualty rate which at Cassino was extremely high.

6. The casualties.

References

Abrahams, Roger D. *Deep Down in the Jungle*. Chicago: Aldine, 1970a.
———. *Positively Black*. Englewood Cliffs, N.J.: Prentice-Hall,1970b.
———. *Talking Black*. Rowley, Mass.: Newbury House, 1976.
———. "Towards a Sociological Theory of Folklore: Performing Services." In
    Robert H. Byington, *Working Americans*, Washington, D.C.: Smithsonian,
    1978, pp. 19–42.
Abrahams, Roger D., Kenneth S. Goldstein, and Wayland D. Hand. *By Land and
    Sea*. Hatboro, Pa.: Legacy Books, 1985.
Almazol, Ed. *Twelve Songs from the Vietnam War*. Cassette tape. Collected from
    an unknown field source by Almazol, formerly a helicopter pilot in B
    Company, 229 Aviation Battalion, attached to the 1st Cavalry Division
    based on An Khe in 1967–68. Vietnam Veterans Oral History and Folklore
    Project, State University College at Buffalo, New York, n.d.
American Red Cross. *The American Red Cross with the Armed Forces*. Washington,
    D.C.: Red Cross, 1945.
Babad, Harry. *Roll Me Over*. New York: Oak Publications, 1972.
Ballard-Reisch, Deborah. " 'China Beach' and 'Tour of Duty': American Tele-
    vision and Revisionist History of the Vietnam War." *Journal of Popular
    Culture*, Vol. 25, No. 3, 135–49, 1991.
Barrett-Litoff, Judy, and David C. Smith. "Will He Get My Letter? Popular
    Portrayals of Mail and Morale During World War II." *Journal of Popular
    Culture*, Vol. 24, No. 4, 21–43, 1990.
Billings, John D. *Hardtack and Coffee: The Unwritten Story of Army Life*. Boston:
    George M. Smith and Co., 1888.
Bodey, Donald. *F.N.G.* New York: Ballantine Books, 1985.

Boyne, Walter J., and Steven L. Thompson. *The Wild Blue*. New York: Ballantine Books, 1986.

Brand, Oscar. *Bawdy Songs and Backroom Ballads*. New York: Dorchester Press, 1960.

Brophy, John, and Eric Partridge. *The Long Trail*. London: Andre Deutsch, 1965.

Broudy, Saul F. *G.I. Folklore in Vietnam*. Tape recording. Music Division Archive, LC (LWO 8644). 1967.

————. "G.I. Folklore in Vietnam." M.A. thesis, University of Pennsylvania, 1969.

Browne, Ray B., and Carlos C. Drake. *A Night with the Hants*. Bowling Green, Ohio: Popular Press, 1976.

Buck, Peter. *The Coming of the Maori*. Wellington: Whitcombe and Tombs, 1949.

Burke, Carol. "Marching to Vietnam." *Journal of American Folklore*, Vol. 102, No. 406, 424–41, 1989.

"Training Songs of Female Soldiers in the '40s." In M. Paul Holsinger and Mary Anne Schofield, *Visions of War: World War II in Popular Literature and Culture*. Bowling Green, Ohio: Popular Press, 1992.

Burke, Kenneth. *Permanence and Change: An Anatomy of Purpose*. Los Altos, Calif.: Hermes Publication, 1954.

Byington, Robert H. *Working Americans*. Washington, D.C.: Smithsonian, 1978.

————. *Tugboating on the Cape Fear River: A Preliminary Ethnographic Sketch*. In Abrahams et al., *By Land and Sea*. Matboro, Pa.: Legacy Books, 1985.

Cleveland, Les. *The Songs We Sang*. Wellington: Editorial Services, 1959.

————. *The Songs We Sang*. LA–3, LP recording. Wellington, New Zealand: Kiwi Records, 1960.

————. *More Songs We Sang*. LA–6, LP recording. Wellington: Kiwi Records, 1961.

————. *The Songs We Sang: Folklore of World War II*. SLC–121, LP recording. Wellington: Reed Pacific Records, 1975.

————. *The Iron Hand: New Zealand Soldiers' Poems from World War 2*. Wellington: Wai-te-ata Press, 1979.

————. *The Songs We Sang: Folklore of World War II*. TC SLC–121, cassette tape. Wellington: Kiwi Pacific Records, 1982.

————. "When They Send the Last Yank Home: Wartime Images of Popular Culture." *Journal of Popular Culture*, Vol. 18, No. 3, 31–36, 1984.

————. "Soldiers' Songs: The Folklore of the Powerless." *New York Folklore*, Vol. XI, 79–87, 1985.

————. "Military Folklore and the Underwood Collection." *New York Folklore*, Vol. XIII, 87–103, 1987.

————. *The Great New Zealand Songbook*. Auckland: Godwit Press, 1991.

Colquhoun, Neil. *New Zealand Folksongs*. Wellington: Reed, 1972.

Commager, Henry Steele. *The Blue and the Gray*. New York: Mentor, 1973.

Coombs, James. "Celebrations: Rituals of Popular Veneration." *Journal of Popular Culture*, Vol. 22, No. 4, 71–77, 1989.

Costello, John. *Love, Sex and War*. London: Collins, 1985.

Cray, Ed. *The Erotic Muse*. London: Anthony Blond, 1969.

————. *The Erotic Muse*. 2nd ed. Urbana: University of Illinois Press, 1992.

Crofut, William. *Troubadour: A Different Battlefield*. New York: E. P. Dutton, 1968.

Dallas, Karl. *The Cruel Wars*. London: Wolfe Publishing, 1972.

Davis, Mike. *Songs of the U.T.T. (Utility Tactical Transport) 1965–66*. Cassette tape. Fayetteville, Ark.: Tuck Boys, Bien Hoa Productions, 1987.

Devilbiss, M. C. "Gender Integration and Unit Deployment: A Study of G.I. Jo." *Armed Forces and Society*, Vol. 1, No. 4, 523–52, 1985.

de Witt, Hugh. *Bawdy Barrack-Room Ballads*. London: Tandem, 1970.

Dickson, Paul. *Chow: A Cook's Tour of Military Food*. New York: New American Library, 1978.

Dolph, Edward A. *Sound Off!* New York: Cosmopolitan Book Corporation, 1929.

Duncan, H. D. *Communication and Social Order*. New York: Bedminster Press, 1962.

Durham, James P. *Songs of S.E.A. (Southeast Asia)*. UP 105, LP recording. Distributor unknown, 1971.

Edwards, Ron. *Index to 1972 Australian Folksong*. Kuranda, Queensland: Ram's Skull Press, 1972a.

———. *Australian Folk Songs*. Holloway's Beach, Queensland: Ram's Skull Press, 1972b.

———. *Australian Bawdy Ballads*. Kuranda: Ram's Skull Press, 1973.

Ellis, John. *Eye-Deep in Hell*. London: Croom Helm, 1976.

Evans, James W., and Gardner L. Harding. *Entertaining the American Army*. New York: Association Press, 1921.

Farwell, Byron. *Mr. Kipling's Army*. New York: W. W. Norton, 1981.

Fish, Lydia M. "General Edward G. Lansdale and the Folksongs of Americans in the Vietnam War." *Journal of American Folklore*, Vol. 102, No. 406, 390–411, 1989.

Fluck, Winifred. "Popular Culture as a Mode of Socialization: A Theory about the Social Functions of Popular Culture Forms." *Journal of Popular Culture*, Vol. 21, No. 3, 31–46, 1987.

Gammage, Bill. *The Broken Years*. Canberra: ANU Press, 1974.

Gaventa, John. *Power and Powerlessness*. Urbana: University of Illinois Press, 1980.

Getz, Charles W. *The Wild Blue Yonder: Songs of the Air Force*. Vol. 1. Burlingame, Calif.: Redwood Press, 1981.

———. *The Wild Blue Yonder: Songs of the Air Force*. Vol. II. Stag Bar Edition. Burlingame: Redwood Press, 1986a.

———. *Songs of the Air Force*. LP record. Burlingame: Redwood Press, 1986b.

Glazer, Tom, ed. *Songs of Peace, Freedom and Protest*. New York: David McKay, 1970.

Gray, J. Glenn. *The Warriors: Reflections on Men in Battle*. New York: Harcourt Brace, 1959.

Green, Archie. *Only a Miner*. Urbana: University of Illinois Press, 1972.

Grinker, Roy R., and John P. Spiegel. *War Neuroses*. Toronto: Blakiston Co., 1945.

Hart, Harold J., ed. *The Complete Immortalia*. New York: Hart Publishing Co., 1971.

Hasford, Gustav. *The Short-Timers*. New York: Bantam Books, 1979.

Henderson, Hamish. *Ballads of World War II*. Glasgow: Lili Marleen Club, c.1945.

Holsinger, M. Paul, and Mary Anne Schofield. *Visions of War: World War II in Popular Literature and Culture*. Bowling Green, Ohio: Popular Press, 1992.

Hopkins, Anthony. *Songs from the Front and Rear*. Edmonton: Hurtig, 1979.

Hurd, Charles. *The Compact History of the American Red Cross*. New York: Hawthorne Books, 1954.

In Country. *Folksongs of Americans in the Vietnam War*. Cassette Tape. Chicago: Flying Fish Records, FF 90552, 1991.

Jackson, Bruce. *Wake Up Dead Man: Afro-American Worksongs from Texas Prisons*. Cambridge, Mass.: Harvard University Press, 1972.

Johnson, Sandee Shaffer. *Cadences: The Jody Call Book*. No. 1. Canton, Ohio: Daring Press, 1983.

Jonas, Dick. FSH Dick Jonas. LP5156, LP recording. Mesilla Park, N.M.: Goldust Records, 1985.

———. *FSH Volume 1*. C–156, cassette tape. Las Cruces, N.M.: Goldust Records, 1987a.

———. *FSH Volume II*. C–157, cassette tape. Las Cruces, N.M.: Goldust Records, 1987b.

———. *Two Sides of Dick Jonas*. C–162, cassette tape. Las Cruces, N.M.: Goldust Records, 1987c.

Junger, Ernst. *The Storm of Steel*. London: Chatto and Windus, 1929.

Karpeles, Maud. *Cecil Sharpe's Collection of English Folk Songs*. Vol. 2. London: Oxford University Press, 1974.

Kenagy, S. G. "Sexual Symbolism in the Language of the Air Force Pilot: A Psychoanalytic Approach to Folk Speech." *Western Folklore*, Vol. 37, No. 2, 89–101, 1978.

Kirst, H. H. *The Lieutenant Must Be Mad*. London: Mayflower Books, 1974.

La Dege, John H. *Merchant Ships: A Pictorial Study*. Cambridge, Md.: Cornell Maritime Press, 1965.

Lahey, John. *Australian Favorite Ballads*. New York: Oak Publications, 1965.

Langer, Suzanne K. *Feeling and Form*. London: Routledge and Kegan Paul, 1953.

Lanning, Michael L. *The Only War We Had*. New York: Ballantine Books, 1987.

Lansdale, Edward G. *LWO 8281* (AFS 17,483 and 18,882). Music Division, LC. (Catalogued as Tapes AFS 17.483 and 18.882). 51 songs in English and Vietnamese, recorded in Saigon during the Vietnam War. 1967.

———. *LWO 9518* (AFS 18,977–18,982). Music Division, LC. 160 songs by U.S. military personnel, Vietnamese singers and various entertainers. Collected by General Lansdale and subsequently edited in the United States, 1976.

Legman, G. *Rationale of the Dirty Joke*. New York: Grove Press, 1968.

———. *No Laughing Matter*. London: Granada Publishing, 1978.

Leo, Juliusz. *Zbiór Pieśni Polskich*. Jerusalem: Ministry of Religion and Education. Printed by the Publishing House of the San Franciscans, 1944.

Levine, Lawrence W. *Black Culture and Black Consciousness*. London: Oxford University Press, 1977.

Loesser, Arthur. *Humor in American Song*. New York: Howell Soskin, 1942.

Lurie, Alison. *The Language of Clothes*. New York: Random House, 1981.

Lynn, Frank. *Songs for Singin'*. San Francisco: Chandler Publishing Co., 1961.

McCarl, Robert S. "Occupational Folklife: A Theoretical Hypothesis." *Western Folklore*, Vol. 37, No. 3, 145–61, 1978.

———. *The District of Columbia Firefighters' Project: A Case Study in Occupational Folklife*. Washington, D.C.: Smithsonian Institution Press, 1985.

McGregor, Craig. *Bawdy Ballads and Sexy Songs*. New York: Belmont/Tower Books, 1972.

Mackay, Arthur, ed. *Immortalia: An Anthology of American Ballads, Sailors' Songs, Cowboy Songs, College Songs, Parodies, Limericks, and Other Humorous Verses and Doggerel*. New York: Karman Society, 1927.

Mauldin, Bill. *Up Front*. New York: Henry Holt, 1944.

Mayo, Katherine. *"That Damn Y."* Boston: Houghton Mifflin, 1931.

Meyer, Michael. "The S.A. Song Literature." *Journal of Popular Culture*, Vol. 11, No. 3, 568–80, 1977.

Narváez, Peter, and Martin Laba. *Media Sense*. Bowling Green, Ohio: Popular Press, 1985.

Nettleingham, F. T. *Tommy's Tunes*. London: Erskine Macdonald, 1917.

Newsom, Jon. *Perspectives on John Philip Sousa*. Washington, D.C.: Library of Congress, 1983.

Niles, John J. *Singing Soldiers*. New York: Scribner's Sons, 1927.

Page, Martin. *Kiss Me Goodnight Sergeant Major*. London: Hart Davis MacGibbon, 1973.

————. *For Gawdsake Don't Take Me*. London: Hart Davis MacGibbon, 1976.

Palmer, Edgar A. *G.I. Songs*. New York: Sheridan House, 1944.

Palmer, Roy. *The Rambling Soldier*. Harmondsworth: Kestrel, 1977.

Parallex. *U.S. Army Infantry*. 491404, cassette tape. Elk Grove, Ill.: Parallex Corporation, 1986a.

————. *U.S. Marines*. Cassette tape, Vol. 1, 491400; Vol. 2, 491401. Elk Grove, Ill.: Parallex Corporation, 1986b.

Partridge, Eric. *A Dictionary of Slang and Unconventional English*. New York: Macmillan, 1970.

Paterson, A. B. *The Old Bush Songs Composed and Sung in the Bushranging, Digging and Overlanding Days*. Sydney: Angus and Robertson, 1905.

Peat, Frank E., and Lee Orian Smith. *Legion Airs*. New York: Leo Feist, 1932.

Posselt, Eric. *Give Out! Songs of, by and for the Men in the Service*. Miami: Granger Books, 1943.

Rathbone, Joseph. *Joseph*. London: Michael Joseph, 1979.

Rich, George W., and David F. Jacobs. "Saltpetre: A Folkloric Adjustment to Stress." *Western Folklore*, Vol. 32, No. 3, 164–79, 1973.

Ross, Angus. *23 Battalion*. Wellington, New Zealand: Internal Affairs Department, 1959.

Sandburg, Carl. *The American Songbag*. New York: Harcourt Brace, 1927.

Santino, Jack. "Characteristics of Occupational Narratives." *Western Folklore*, Vol. 37, No. 3, 202, 1978.

————. "Yellow Ribbons and Seasonal Flags: The Folk Assemblage of War." *Journal of American Folklore*, Vol. 105, No. 415, 19–33, 1992.

Scaff, William. *Bong Son Blues*. Cassette tape of items recorded in Vietnam. Monrovia, Calif.: Little Sun, 1987.

Sharpe, Cecil W. "The Sailor and the Soldier." *Journal of the Folksong Society*, Vol. 5, 72–73, 1914.

Silverman, Jerry. *Folk Song Encyclopedia*. New York: Chappell Music Co., 1975.

————. *The Dirty Songbook*. New York: Stein and Day, 1982.

Slotkin, Richard. *The Fatal Environment*. New York: Atheneum, 1985.

Smith, Franklin D. *Songs with Hash Marks*. LP recording. Phoenix, Ariz.: Council on Abandoned Military Posts, n.d.

Sossaman, Stephen. "More on Pleiku Jackets in Vietnam." *Journal of American Folklore*, Vol. 102, No. 403, 76, 1989.

Stoffregen, Goetz Otto. *Deutsches Soldatenliederbuch*. Berlin: E. S. Mitler and Son, 1943.

Tate, Brad. *The Bastard from the Bush*. Australian Folklore Occasional Paper No. 11. Kuranda, Queensland: Ram's Skull Press, 1982.

Thompson, Stith. *Motif-Index of Folk Literature*. Bloomington: Indiana University Press, 1955.

Thorpe, Peter. "Buying the Farm: Notes on the Folklore of the Modern Military Aviator." *Northwest Folklore*, Vol. 11, No. 1, 11–17, 1967.

Tinsley, Jim Bob. *He Was Singin' This Song*. Orlando: University of Florida, 1981.

Tuso, Joseph F. "Folksongs of the American Fighter Pilot in Southeast Asia, 1967–68." In *Folklore Forum*, No. 7. Bloomington, Ind: Folklore Forum Society, 1971.

———. *Singing the Vietnam Blues*. College Station: Texas A and M University Press, 1990.

Underwood, Agnes M. "Folklore from G.I. Joe." *New York Folklore Quarterly*, Vol. III, No. 4, 286–97, 1947.

Van Creveld, Martin. *Technology and War*. New York: Free Press, 1989.

Wallrich, William. *Air Force Airs*. New York: Duell, Sloan and Pearce, 1957.

———. "Superstition and the Air Force." *Western Folklore*, Vol. 19, No. 1, 11–16, 1960.

Ward, Russel. *The Australian Legend*. London: Oxford, 1964.

Ward-Jackson, C. H. *Airman's Song Book*. London: Sylvan Press, 1945.

———. *Airman's Song Book*. 2nd ed. London: Blackwood, 1967.

Warner, Lloyd. *The Living and the Dead*. New Haven, Conn.: Yale University Press, 1959.

Wesley Ward, C. *Barracks Ballads*. Franklin, Ind.: Astronautics Publishing Co., 1966.

Westmoreland, William C. *A Soldier Reports*. New York: Dell Publishing Co., 1976.

White, John I. *Git Along Little Dogies*. Urbana: University of Illinois Press, 1975.

Williams, J. P. "All's Fair in Love and Journalism: Female Rivalry in Superman." *Journal of Popular Culture*, Vol. 24, No. 2, 103–12, 1990.

Winstock, Lewis. *Songs and Music of the Redcoats*. London: Leo Cooper, 1970.

Winterich, John T. *Squads Write!* New York: Harper and Brothers, 1931.

York, Dorothea. *Mud and Stars*. New York: Henry Holt, 1931.

Zweig, Arnold. *The Case of Sergeant Grischa*. London: Panther, 1961.

Subject Index

Index of Song Titles

Index of First Lines

About the Author

LES CLEVELAND is now retired, having taught at Victoria University of Wellington, New Zealand. He is the author of numerous books, including, most recently, *The Great New Zealand Songbook* (1991).

DATE DUE			
APR 04 1998			